WHY
KAREN CARPENTER
MATTERS

Music
Matters

Evelyn McDonnell

Series Editor

WHY KAREN CARPENTER MATTERS

Karen Tongson

UNIVERSITY OF TEXAS PRESS
AUSTIN

Project editors: Lynne Chapman and Amanda Frost
Cover design: Amanda Weiss
Typeset in Knockout and Fournier by Dustin Kilgore
Book cover printed by Phoenix Color, interior by Sheridan Books

Requests for permission to reproduce material
from this work should be sent to:

Permissions
University of Texas Press
P.O. Box 7819
Austin, TX 78713-7819
utpress.utexas.edu/rp-form

♾ The paper used in this book meets the minimum requirements of
ANSI/NISO Z39.48-1992 (R1997) (Permanence of Paper).

Library of Congress Cataloging-in-Publication Data
Names: Tongson, Karen, author.
Title: Why Karen Carpenter matters / Karen Tongson.
Description: Austin : University of Texas Press, 2019. | Series: Music matters
Identifiers: LCCN 2018039812
ISBN 978-1-4773-1884-3 (pbk. : alk. paper)
ISBN 978-1-4773-1885-0 (library e-book)
ISBN 978-1-4773-1886-7 (non-library e-book)
Subjects: LCSH: Carpenter, Karen, 1950-1983. | Singers—United
States—Biography.
Classification: LCC ML420.C2564 T65 2019 | DDC 782.42164092—dc23
LC record available at https://lccn.loc.gov/2018039812

doi:10.7560/318843

To José Esteban Muñoz (1967–2013)
for pointing me to the queer horizon

CONTENTS

PREFACE

Unlike many other young icons of rock and pop lost to overdoses under dramatic circumstances, from Janis Joplin to Jimi Hendrix to Jim Morrison, Karen Carpenter faded out slowly, just like the music she and her brother, Richard, were known for making together as the Carpenters. One might even describe her death in 1983 as a protracted suicide aided by her underconsumption—the refusal to eat and nourish her body—as opposed to the raucous excesses and overconsumption so characteristic of other rock stars' stories of demise. In this book, I revisit the events of Karen's life and death, not in an effort to retrace history or to speculate on how this could have happened, but instead to explore the different afterlives generated by her music and her voice in far-flung settings, including in our fantasy worlds. Karen Carpenter matters, I argue, because she transformed—because *we* transformed—the uneventful in her life, work, and even death into something extraordinary.

Volumes of work—biographies, academic articles, think pieces before such things as "think pieces" existed—have been devoted to the Carpenters, the brother-sister duo whose storied rise to the top of the charts, and the top of the world, coincided with Richard Nixon's America and a worldview that staunchly held on to an attitude of Sunbelt optimism, despite the international and domestic turmoil caused by the Vietnam War. *Why Karen Carpenter Matters* delves into some of the scenes of the Carpenters' suburban upbringing while bringing an international outlook to their story and their musical body of work. I focus on Karen Carpenter, and not the duo known as the Carpenters, precisely because it is *Karen's* iconicity—due in no small part to her tragic, early death and haunting contralto voice—that resulted in their music's enduring appeal in the United States and abroad. This book delves not only into the band's movements through time and space, but more specifically into the myths surrounding Karen Carpenter's voice, which eventually became reanimated through other bodies and other voices, in the Philippines (my birthplace) and elsewhere, through brown bodies, queer bodies, differently abled bodies.

All this said, this book is not a comprehensive biography or even an extended social history about Karen or the Carpenters and every album they recorded or every venue where they may have performed. There are lengthier, more extensive volumes to turn to for that level of thoroughness. Instead, this book, like so much of my other work, is inspired by something the Victorian aesthete and writer Walter Pater once wrote in the preface to his 1873 book *The Renaissance*. He asks, "What is this song or picture, this engaging personality presented in life or in a book, to *me*? What effect does it really produce on me?"

A good portion of this book is devoted to answering Pater's questions about music, lives, and engaging personalities, and exploring why Karen Carpenter matters *to me*. You see, my Filipino musician parents named me after Karen Carpenter in 1973. Karen is my namesake,[1] and her voice and music are coordinates in the musical mapping of my family's journeys across the Pacific, between big cities like Manila and the sprawl of Southern California, and between old-fashioned notions of romance and the queer desires that come to the surface despite the Carpenters' milquetoast musical fantasies about "normal" love.

Karen Carpenter matters to me because I was nurtured on the idea that my mother, who is also a singer, sounded like Karen Carpenter. My mother christened me Karen when I was born in Manila, five years before we sought our fortunes in the United States for the first time. Karen Carpenter is, at once, my blessing and my burden.

The Philippines is often depicted as a kind of sonic mirror of the United States because of its robust history of cover bands who imitated American pop styles ever since the US "liberated" the island nation in World War II. The relationship between American and Filipino pop culture is an intimate one because of the US military presence in the country and the influence of media like the Armed Forces Radio on the nation's taste and entertainment culture.

Karen Carpenter matters to Filipinos and Filipino Americans like me, whose movements through the megalopolis of Manila, to and from the Philippines' rural provinces, and eventually to distant places for overseas labor, are scored to Karen's voice: one redolent of tears, even when she sings about unbridled joy. *Why Karen Carpenter Matters*, in other words, is not about why others have thought the Carpenters mattered as an American pop group who helped spawn soft rock (though this fact is of the utmost importance), or as the most avowedly "goody-four-shoes" pop act to rule the charts. Instead, *Why Karen Carpenter Matters* is about why Karen matters to people of color, immigrants, queer people, gender outlaws, and everyone other than the white Nixon-era suburbanites she and her music are said to have represented. In order to make this case, the book reaches through and between real and conjured histories, memories false and true, born of cross-cultural tales of affection, aggression, and an abiding longing.

Why Karen Carpenter Matters will move between the Southern California suburbs, where the duo's signature "Spectrum sound" was cultivated amidst chain stores and defense plants (like the one Agnes Carpenter, Karen's mother, worked in), and the Philippines, where I was bestowed with the name Karen. Southern California's suburbs became my own family's destination, inspired in part by a dream of "yesterdays once more"—the radio traces of a good life that has since receded into memory, or perhaps never was. Combining memoir with history, critical and creative geographies, musical analysis, queer theory, and on occasion, self-analysis, *Why Karen Carpenter Matters* explores the ties that bind artists and listeners beyond families and fandoms.

– 1 –

WHITENESS AND PROMISES

On February 4, 1983, Karen Carpenter died of complications from anorexia nervosa while she was reaching for a fuzzy bathrobe in the bedroom closet at her parents' mid-century suburban home in Downey, California. By all accounts—Ray Coleman's 1994 biography chief among them—Karen spent the day before she died cruising between suburban chain stores, looking for sturdy household items like a washer-dryer at the Downey Gemco, a big-box store absorbed by Target in the mid-1980s that she affectionately referred to as "the Gucci of Downey." She ate a shrimp salad for dinner with her parents at Bob's Big Boy and picked up a couple of tacos to go from a local joint next door so she could snack on them while indulging in the made-for-TV spectacle of a manscaped, micro-kimono-clad Richard Chamberlain in *Shogun*. Everyone thought she was on the mend, the very picture of SoCal suburbanity in repose, eating tacos and watching the tube all night, before what was supposed to be another sunshiny day in an endless season—nay, a lifetime—of sunniness.

On the other side of the Pacific, a mere stone's throw from the land of *Shogun* and newfangled devices like sing-along karaoke machines, I learned about Karen Carpenter's death in the waiting room of a dubious travel agency in Little Ongpin, Manila's old Chinatown district. I was nine years old, stuck there with my musician parents. They were making arrangements for our departure from the Philippines, where I was born, to the dry heat of Southern California, where my white stepfather grew up just fifty miles east of Downey in a region called the Inland Empire: a place with its own aerospace and defense plants nestled between the citrus groves and the stucco.

Karen Carpenter Dies at 32 screamed the newsprint just above the fold of a Filipino newspaper discarded on the cracked, moist Naugahyde bench next to me. Even though my body had slackened while I was sweating it out in the tropical density of that miserable waiting room, cooled only intermittently by a half-cocked electric fan, my spine went stiff as soon as my eyes grazed that headline. '*SusMaryosep!* I cursed in my head.[1] *My namesake is dead.* And she died young—at 32, a year younger than Jesus himself.

At nine going on ten, I was just growing into my fear of mortality, which was aggravated by the fact that we were about to take another epic, transpacific journey on a jet packed with people chain-smoking duty-free Dunhills. At least this was how I remembered my first flight to the States when I was five. I also recalled the oxygen masks dropping somewhere past Guam, and my mother setting her half-drawn cigarette in the tiny armrest ashtray before strapping a mask over my face.

My family, comprising mostly professional musicians, made a lot out of the fact that I was named after Karen Carpenter instead of a relative, saint, or some other Catholic luminary. My grandfather and his brothers—Romy Katindig and the Hi-Chords—were credited with innovating Latin jazz in the Philippines in the 1950s and '60s. My mom, whose stage name is Maria, carried on the family business, briefly singing in OPM (original Pilipino music) acts in the 1970s with supergroups like Counterpoint and the Circus Band, before falling in love and forming a touring jazz combo with my stepfather: a California-born, Hawaii-based musician named Jimmie Dykes. His Pacific Rim roots landed him gigs with some of the top Filipino performers of the 1970s, including one of my mom's godfathers, crooner Roberto "Bert" Nievera from the Society of Seven.

My mother's voice was often compared to Karen Carpenter's when both of them were in their prime, so Karen was like family—but more of a distant relative whose resemblance felt significant even if it was only circumstantial, and whose global accomplishments were touted as aspirational for my musical clan: Karen Carpenter, superstar.

Even before she died in 1983, Karen fulfilled something of a spiritual role in our home in Manila, like the friendly ghosts our neighborhood *curandera* claimed to have found living in our duhat tree, and with whom my grandmother

Linda Katindig tried to negotiate one evening after several hours of mahjong and too many bottles of San Miguel beer. She asked the mother-daughter spirits not to manifest in front of us lest they actually scare us to death, even as she acknowledged and respected their own claims to residency and tacitly accepted their ubiquity. Karen, too, was everywhere: in the late-night sing-alongs around the water-damaged upright piano on the veranda, in the cook's whistled refrains of "Top of the World," and in my name. But most of the time, as the song goes, it was just the radio.

I challenge anyone visiting the Philippines, now or then, to try to last a day—nay, several hours—without hearing a Carpenters song on the radio, or in a karaoke establishment, or performed by a cover band. Though there aren't any charts to prove definitively that the Carpenters were more popular in the Philippines than in any other nation in the world, their enduring presence on Filipino radio, and in Filipino American karaoke repertoires, attests to my people's profound affinity with this most wholesome of American duos. After all, the Carpenters famously crooned at Nixon's White House during West German Chancellor Willy Brandt's state visit, while our neighbors in Southeast Asia were ablaze in napalm and our own would-be dictator, Ferdinand Marcos, was declaring martial law. Their *Now and Then* album from 1973, the same year my teen parents (who met performing in a Manila concert production of *Jesus Christ Superstar*) christened me Karen, has been clocked by Tom Smucker as "one of the greatest pop music explorations of whiteness in the last half century."[2]

The Carpenters' westward migration from New Haven, Connecticut, to Downey, California, a white, working-class suburb conveniently situated between Orange County and Los Angeles, would seem to affirm this narrow trajectory toward "whiteness and promises," to invoke a Filipino karaoke machine that misinterpreted the line about "white lace and promises" in "We've Only Just Begun." Both the original lyric and the error are essentially referring to the same thing: an American suburban fantasy of the good life, with a good wife, "sharing horizons that are new *to us*," but not foreign or strange in the grander scheme of things. Familiar. Comfortable. Just as things should be. Or at least as we always pretend we want them to be. As Smucker writes, "Control and precision—often assigned as white musical values—and elaborate pop production that implies a kind of mass affluence, locate the Carpenters' soft rock in the suburban world abstracted on the *Now & Then* album cover."

It's easy enough now for scholars, historians, and music critics like Smucker to point out with twenty-twenty hindsight how harmless the Carpenters were, implying that Karen, Richard, and their team were blithely unselfconscious about the incompatibility of their "goody-four-shoes" image with the zenith of late-1960s counterculture. The Carpenters came to prominence during a particularly tumultuous era in the United States, both musically and politically. In the wake of the summer of love, Woodstock, and the escalation of the war in Vietnam, Karen's voice—described by detractors as "saccharine" and championed by others as distinctly "smooth" or "velvety"—began to dominate the airwaves with both nostalgic reflections and optimistic projections about better times crafted from "only yesterdays." Mired in the Watergate scandal and with his days in office numbered, Richard Nixon took the opportunity to take a break from his legal and political woes to describe the duo as "young America at its best."

Richard Carpenter chafed at the creepy wholesomeness of their image, and in particular at how A&M records marketed the duo in soft-focus, vaguely romantic poses among jutting rocks on picturesque seashores. "[The *Close to You* cover] looks like a Valentine's card. We're not sweethearts," he complained in a 2002 BBC documentary, *Close to You: The Story of the Carpenters*. Sure, the music itself is mostly romantic, from the first blush of affection's wanton anthropomorphism in "(They Long to Be) Close to You," to enduring love's auspicious commencement in "We've Only Just Begun." But the messengers, Richard insisted—felt he had to insist—were not.

In the same BBC documentary, John Bettis, Richard's lyricist and songwriting partner, unabashedly declared that in 1970, the year the Carpenters first topped the charts, "Everybody was dying to be something they weren't. Everybody was dying to be from the ghetto. Everybody was dying to not be from the suburbs. The fact of the matter was that we were who we were, and we were white, middle-class American kids. And we wrote like that, sang like that; we dressed like that; we lived like that."[3]

* * *

Needless to say, my musical family was not—is not—like that, despite the belated addition of my Southern Californian stepfather to the mix. By the time I was born, in 1973, the Katindigs were genteel, post-provincial, post–World War II Manileños, or Manila-dwelling prototypes for what we now call the *bourgeois-bohème*: hedonistic artists with some capitalist success and an aspirational, rather spendy sensibility. Unlike the middle-class American white kids, who Bettis speculates are drawn to the authenticating grit of a "ghetto" past, the Katindigs made every effort to transpose their war-torn, provincial Pampangan origins, and their scrappy upbringing in the working-class Manila neighborhood of Obrero, Tondo, into a hip, internationalist Latin-jazz sound for the finest lounges and cocktail bars of southeast Asia and even the United States.

In 1970, the year the Carpenters released their first number-one single, "(They Long to Be) Close to You," my grandfather Romy Katindig and his brothers, the Hi-Chords, were performing regularly in Las Vegas. As his younger brother, Eddie, the vibraphone and sax player who eventually came to be known as "the Kenny G of the

Philippines," noted in an interview for a book called *Pinoy Jazz Traditions*: "This was about 1969, and we were playing all over America for four years. We would do a lot of shows. We fronted for Count Basie's Big Band and also for Peter Nero. The Tropicana Hotel in Las Vegas was one of our *puestos* [regular venues]."[4]

The Carpenters played the nearby Sands and Riviera, and part of me wonders if either family ensemble ever noticed the other gigging on the strip, even unconsciously, in passing. At the very least, I fantasize that my grandfather knew and cared about who the Carpenters were and would keep an eye out because his teenage daughter was such a huge fan. But as with most things having to do with this charming man, his attentiveness to his daughter's interests, especially from half a world away, is likelier to have flourished in fantasy than in reality.

My grandmother, who remained in the Philippines with my mom and my uncle during Romy's years on the road, was a highly educated mestiza from Iloilo in the Visayas. Linda Oñas was born to Juan Oñas, a US naval officer of Spanish-Filipino descent, and his devoutly Catholic wife, Salud. My great-grandfather Juan died of tuberculosis before World War II, leaving Salud to raise their two daughters, Linda and Mellie, on her own. Together these three fled through Visayan rice fields, ducking Japanese bullets, while concealing the ceremonial American flag bequeathed to Salud by the US Navy after Juan's death. She eventually dismantled the stars and stripes, both burdensome and dangerous in her possession, and repurposed the fabric as school dresses for my grandmother and great-aunt during the colonial occupation.

After the war, the Oñas women moved to Manila, where my grandmother, Linda, met Romy Katindig in the early 1950s. She fancied herself a gal about town because she held an urbane secretarial job—think Peggy Olson in *Mad Men*—of which she was particularly proud. Romy, whose given name, Romeo, is entirely too apt, was the pianist and arranger for a radio show that recorded live in the big city park, Luneta, now Rizal, Park—near my grandmother's corporate office. They met during one of her lunch breaks, and though she was suspicious of his caddish charms, they eventually ended up marrying in a proper Catholic wedding at Salud's insistence after my mother had already been conceived.

My mom—christened Elizabeth before she adopted her stage name, Maria, for the business called "show"—inherited my grandmother's poised mestiza femininity and my grandfather's drive for musical adventure and stardom. When we first visited the Southern California suburbs in 1978, about five years before we would eventually settle there, I could tell she was disoriented by not moving easily through this new environment with an air of specialness and privilege. She possessed, if not exactly whiteness, a light-skinned middle-classness that she and my grandmother wielded so well in Manila, only to be confronted in Riverside, California, with a working-class American suburban whiteness neither of us quite understood, let alone knew how to navigate.

My mother was stunned when the neighborhood kids encircled me on her soon-to-be mother-in-law's neatly clipped lawn to ask what I was, where I came from, and whether or not I was Christian. When I responded that I was Filipino and Catholic, these nasty little inquisitors asked if I "ate people" and knew how to use a toilet. They also told me, "Catholics aren't Christians." Evangelical Christianity at its densest.

My white soon-to-be-grandmother, Marion Dykes, shooed them away with a sternness and gravitas I came to understand later as a holdover from her deeply ingrained midcentury decency. I appreciated her sense of decorum in those kinds of situations though I never could keep my elbows properly off the table during dinners at her home, which usually involved stewed tomatoes and other items peculiar to my young Filipino palate, with my preference for the charred, fatty parts of grilled meats.

My mother was only fifteen in 1970 when the Carpenters' album *Close to You* went platinum in the United States and across the globe. She began to sing their repertoire in her earliest coed vocal groups around the same time. These groups were inspired stylistically by the Carpenters' cultivation of a pop choral sound, which could be described as next-level Fifth Dimension: more complex key changes, and more intricate jazz harmonies, which matched well with my mother's own musical heritage. By the time I was born, several years later, my namesake, Karen, and the Carpenters were ensconced firmly at the top of the charts, and my mother too hit her stride in her career.

From 1970 to 1973, the Carpenters had notched hit album after hit album, from their eponymous 1971 follow-up to *Close to You* to my soundtrack in utero, the 1972 masterpiece *A Song for You*, which boasted some of their most enduring original hits, including "Top of the World," "Hurting Each Other," "Goodbye to Love," and "I Won't Last a Day without You." Mom's singing career was derailed ever so slightly by my impending birth and a brief, tumultuous marriage to my biological father, a tenor named Henry Tongson, who also adored Karen Carpenter's voice. It was inevitable I'd be baptized as Karen by these eighteen-year-old parents and superfans who met singing in the Circus Band, one of Manila's hottest acts, known for performing more than the occasional Carpenters cover.

Once *this* Karen made her way into the world, into a Manila newly under the thumb of Ferdinand Marcos's martial law, the Oñas matriarchy, which was reconstituted in the late 1960s after Romy Katindig absconded with one of his overseas lovers, circled the wagons. My grandmother, my great-grandmother, and my great-aunt helped raise me (as they had raised my mom), while Maria took a choice gig performing nightly at a tony supper club called the Top of the Hilton with the Carding Cruz band. It was several years into her residency at "the Top" that she met Jimmie Dykes, the musical director for Bert Nievera's touring show, who shared the bill with her act for the better part of a year. Like my mother's father, her younger brother, and the self-described "Piano Picker," Richard Carpenter, Jimmie was a pianist and arranger. By 1977, just as the Carpenters seemed to be losing their platinum magic with experimental forays into proggy futurism, like "Calling Occupants of Interplanetary Craft (The Recognized Anthem of World Contact Day)," my mom and soon-to-be-stepdad were taking copious couple photos around Manila's landmarks in matching astrology tees and denim bell bottoms—he's a Leo, she's an Aries. Unbeknownst to me—I was barely past toddlerdom at the time—our own westward trajectory to the Southern California suburbs was being set into motion, and they wanted to remember Manila when they left.

* * *

In Carpenters lore, Harold and Agnes Carpenter moved to Southern California in 1963 to jumpstart Richard's musical career. Karen and Richard's cousin, Joan Pennisi, verifies this in another BBC documentary, this one from 2007, *The Carpenters' Story: Only Yesterdays*: "I think Richard's parents, Agnes and Harold, were beginning to feel that Richard really had talent, and there's two places you should go if you have musical talent: either New York or California." Noticeably irked by the foregrounding of his personal ambitions in accounts of the family's relocation, Richard complained in the same documentary: "The story is that they moved here to further my career, but the number-one reason is that my dad wanted to get the hell out of the cold!" Both well-known Carpenters biographers, Ray Coleman and Randy Schmidt, corroborate Richard's protestations, though it's clear his career potential could never quite be subtracted from any of the family's equations. As Schmidt writes, "In addition to their quest for a milder climate, the Carpenter parents saw California—and especially Hollywood—as a place where Richard's dreams of becoming a famous pianist would have a better chance of coming true."[5]

Karen, who was thirteen at the time of their California sojourn, wasn't particularly keen on leaving behind her close-knit circle of friends and cousins in New Haven, Connecticut. Despite the debilitating stage fright we've come to associate with Karen at the height of the Carpenters' stardom, she was by all accounts a socially gregarious child and adolescent in New Haven, and she preferred more robust amusements than her introverted music-geek brother. She remarked once in an interview, "While Richard was listening to music in the basement, I was out playing baseball and football, and playing with my machine gun! I was very tomboyish, quite a character I hear."[6] Her friends, family, and neighbors described Karen as a freewheeling tomboy who reveled in roughhousing outdoors and playing with plastic weaponry instead of dolls. In a middle-school autobiography assignment she wrote right before their big move to California, Karen proudly recounted how she acquired a nasty injury after falling from a trapeze when she was little.[7] She even maintained a morning paper route to earn extra spending money, which Richard noted was "different."[8]

Poking fun at his own dorky, physically inept image—"bad knees" and all—Richard's solo number "Piano Picker," from their 1972 album *A Song for You*, flips the script of his teenage abjection by explaining how his lack of athleticism is why he became such a consummate pianist:

> *Yes, after years and years of practice*
> *And a case of real bad knees*
> *While the other guys were out playin' with the football*
> *I was home bangin' on the keys*

The Carpenter siblings' modest, if strangely frequent, confessions of adolescent gender nonconformity draw little commentary from most biographers and cultural observers.

There is, however, the notable exception of filmmaker Todd Haynes's campy insinuations about the duo's perversity in his experimental video, shot entirely with Barbie dolls, *Superstar: The Karen Carpenter Story* (1987). Richard successfully sued Haynes for copyright infringement, driving the film underground, where it accrued cult status through its illicit circulation and consumption. Beyond the question of copyright, Haynes and his cowriter, Cynthia Schneider, obviously touched a nerve, one barely subcutaneous, radiating with a familiar ache to queer listeners and fans of the Carpenters, like me. Simply put, there's something totally queer about the Carpenters, beyond the mere fact of Karen's tomboyish youth or penchant for percussion. Beyond Richard's preference for "bangin' on the keys" instead of "playin' with . . . girlfriends." Beyond, even, the missteps in A&M's marketing, which implicitly framed the siblings as sweethearts.

Haynes's film begins by asking how a "smooth-voiced girl from Downey, California, led a raucous nation smoothly into the '70s." In its opening sequences, scored to the song the film is named after, "Superstar," Haynes's camera guides us across Southern California's subdivided tracts of ranch-style homes, capacious carports, and three-car garages. The film invites a deeper look not only at the psychological forces behind Karen Carpenter's untimely death but also at the unseemly analog grit of the white working-class suburbs southeast of Los Angeles in which she eventually came of age: a landscape of "grainy days and Mondays," as film scholar Lucas Hilderbrand describes in his article on *Superstar*'s bootleg aesthetics.[9] Haynes's film creatively speculates about the Carpenter family's pathologies, from their mother's controlling nature to Karen's anorexia nervosa to whispers about Richard's "private life" and sexuality.

One needn't even raise the question about whether Richard or Karen were ever gay—ample evidence points to the fact that they were not—to understand how very *queerly* their aberrant normalcy might resonate with others who might also feel fearful of making mistakes in such a master-planned scenario, others for whom one wrong move could undo everything so carefully wrought, so hard won.

"It takes a long time for it to sink in. There are all these habits you've been brought up with all your life. You don't just go plowing through the store buying everything you like," Richard explained after describing his and Karen's stunned response to their first massive royalty check after the success of *Close to You*.[10] The Carpenters' working-class upbringing—and the accompanying sense that it could all go away at any moment without the next hit, the next perfectly calibrated melody, the next sold-out tour—resulted in an anxious perfectionism in their recording practice that was most succinctly captured in an item for the *Southeast News* in 1971. On the eve of their release of "Hurting Each Other," reporter Dan Armstrong visited the duo in the studio as they fine-tuned aspects of the recording that, to his ear, were barely detectable: "To the average listener the song was already completed, and even those of us watching and listening were unable to perceive why the Carpenters would suddenly stop, say 'no that's not right,' and start over again."[11]

KAREN: I want to make the "We ares" huge.
RICHARD: They are huge.
KAREN: I want to make them huger.[12]

Ironically, the queerest thing about the Carpenters, who were once asked point-blank in a phone interview by a

Toronto DJ if their songs were about incest—"I know that Karen's singin' 'em to you. I know they're about incest. You want to talk about this?"[13]—is their exacting normalcy and polished exemplarity. A "nothing remarkable to see here" finely tuned into the thing a lot of people aren't even consciously aware they desire most. In other words, making "easy listening" wasn't easy. And being the poster girl for pop music normalcy would guarantee Karen herself could never lead a normal life, whatever that means. The insistence with which the word *normal* crops up, particularly from Karen's mouth, as their careers reach a certain plateau in the mid-1970s, is telling; it's like a wishful incantation meant to bring something into being through its mere utterance. But as with love, the kind of deep, enduring, and sometimes even infuriating love sung to life in Karen's voice, normalcy could only exist in song, in the shadow world of performance.

Early in the Carpenters' career, in the white heat of their fame, the press surrounding them was decidedly mixed. For every puff piece manufactured by the A&M publicity machine in outlets like *Teen* magazine, there were profiles and reviews that ranged from the merely skeptical to the outright snide and scathing. The legendary *Rolling Stone* critic Lester Bangs famously lambasted the Carpenters and their fans as "creeps" in his review of their sold-out concert in San Diego in 1971. Chief among his complaints was that the band's stage presence lacked a focal point, especially with Karen singing from behind a massive drum set: "She just doesn't give you much to look at, lovely and outgoing as she is."[14]

Bangs's remarks strike me as sexist, insofar as the burden is placed on Karen, the lone woman on stage—"lovely and outgoing as she is"—to give audience members something to look at. This "problem" of having Karen behind the drums would continue to dog the Carpenters until she finally relented and assumed her proper place as a lead singer in the spotlight at the front of the stage. Perhaps Karen had Lester Bangs's *Rolling Stone* review in mind when she answered Johnny Carson's question on *The Tonight Show* about whether or not she "missed sittin' back there" at the drums: "They finally got the message across that they wanted me to get up. I was the only girl in the group, so they were looking at me."[15]

The dispersal of attention away from the lead singer to an amorphous group, which broke with the conventions of live rock stadium performances, prompted Bangs to declare that the Carpenters and their large backing ensemble were an "odd and disjunct congregation." The group made Bangs's girlfriend (his date to the show) "nervous." Especially onerous to the couple was Richard's hokey, mechanical stage presence. Bangs mocks the pianist for lacking emotional depth despite his technical expertise: "In quiet numbers when the lighting was subdued and he was twinkling out pearly arpeggios, he would stare up and off into space with mournful almost-crossed eyes as passionate as Chopin in the throes of creation."[16]

Though Bangs's review is on the more colorful, extreme end of criticism about the Carpenters, it underscores the fact that much of the backlash and ill will harbored against the duo was bound up with their rigorous and workmanlike approach to a style of music that was supposed to go down easy. Such impressions stemmed in part from various reporters' close encounters with the band's protective managerial entourage, as well as the Carpenters' meticulous performance prep and recording practices, which took time away from more in-depth interviews.

Ken Michaels's profile of the Carpenters for the *Chicago Tribune Magazine* in 1971 shrewdly captures at once the frenzy and disaffection of the duo's preparations for their Hollywood Bowl debut. He embeds a paragraph from A&M's publicity sheet in the middle of his own frustrated journalistic efforts to get to the "real Carpenters," as a form of indictment by contrast: "Meet the Carpenters—A&M Records' young brother-sister hitmakers whose gentle harmony, wholesome image and natural unpretentious personalities have virtually crashed thru to make them the nation's No. 1 recording team."[17]

Michaels, meanwhile, is thoroughly handled by the Carpenters' publicity crew, as he struggles to wrangle the duo for a brief interview amidst Richard's frazzled micromanagement of rehearsals and sound checks, his "All-American shoulders tossing under a worried boyish face." Michaels characterizes Karen as mopey, sad, and aloof, with the gaunt visage of an "Unhappy Jane

Wyman."[18] Throughout Michaels's profile, the Carpenters come off as automatons shielded by the swirl of compensatory gregariousness from their retinue of side musicians, hairstylists, roadies, and gofers. Michaels even attributes the awkward, slow-building standing ovation at the end of their Hollywood Bowl debut to Karen's hairdresser, who "accomplishes Mission Impossible" by "pounding her palms together . . . giving filthy, resentful looks to anybody who dares remain seated, which is everybody."[19]

The only thing that briefly punctures Michaels's cynicism about this famous duo of disaffected "kids" zipping in late to all the venues in their not-so-unpretentious Maserati, is hearing Karen sing "For All We Know" during a sound check: "Karen makes us *believe* it. She feels it, the sound system issues it superbly, everything is right. A mood is created, everybody forgets everything except the singer and the song."[20]

The Karen effect: the capacity to make you feel something, to make you *believe* in a spiritual undoing and trembling beneath the polished arpeggios and vacuum-sealed harmonies. In many respects, detractors like Bangs were right. The Carpenters were a little bit creepy, at least in a musical sense. Rhythmically, they were almost always too squarely on the beat, leaving little room for falling behind in a soulful rubato. Their 1973 cover of Leon Russell's "This Masquerade" makes that painfully apparent, lending the song an odd cheeriness despite its minor modality and depressing account of a relationship that's just going through the motions. Richard's arrangements are, like the streets of Disneyland that provide the setting for their "Please Mr. Postman" video, disturbingly clean. As chief gearhead and maestro, Richard was so familiar with the minutiae of each of their recordings that he could clock which turntables at which radio stations ran fast or slow when they broadcast the band's hits.

You can't help but wonder to what extent this trying too hard—this strained effort beneath what is supposed to sound and appear effortless—is symptomatic of their deeply ingrained class aspirations. After all, Agnes and Harold Carpenter settled on the "wrong side of the tracks" in south Downey and were warned that doing so might not bode well for their future mobility.[21] Jerry Dunphy, the legendary Los Angeles newscaster who inspired both Ted Baxter on *The Mary Tyler Moore Show* and Kent Brockman on *The Simpsons*, visited the Carpenters' home for a local TV special in 1972, just as several renovations were underway after Richard and Karen's first major chart triumphs. Dunphy explains that despite all of the duo's smashing successes, "they still live at home with their parents in the not especially fashionable community of Downey." Karen and Richard commented on how their working-class parents did everything they could to invest in their musical needs—from new electric pianos to drum sets, quality microphones, and tape recorders—but sometimes they simply "couldn't swing it."

Harold and Agnes could barely work enough hours to keep up with their bills, but through pluck, persistence, and hard work, they were able to carve out their own version of a suburban paradise in Downey, enabled by their children's accomplishments—the gold records, the concerts at Carnegie, the Royal Albert Hall, and the Hollywood Bowl—as the cover of *Now and Then* immortalizes in its trifold spread.

*   *   *

I wanted our home, our life, to look as neat and glossy as the one that butterflied open so splendidly on the cover of that Carpenters album. Covetous of their neatly clipped lawn—ours was often weedy and overgrown—I also fantasized about the tidiness within that home, and about what would undoubtedly be unblemished, brand-new furniture gleaming with Pledge in each of the rooms.

Our own suburban life was marred by my musician parents' well-intended but ill-equipped efforts to "keep house," something they never really had to do on the road, gigging at five-star hotels with turndown service, or living with my middle-class family in the Philippines, equipped with a full staff of nannies and other help. Their work ethic was a completely different species of hustle from Harold and Agnes Carpenter's, and as a child I couldn't experience it as anything other than aberrant, when all I wanted, desperately, was to be "normal"—to fit in with our new surroundings.

My nightly communion with the Fingerhut catalogue filled me with longing for the spoils of the suburban good life, or at least the installment-plan, mail-order version of it. Canopied beds, sensible rugs, and stealth storage systems to conceal the chaos and detritus of the everyday became the stuff of fantasy for me amidst the piles of musical equipment, cords, charts, and stray percussion instruments that intermingled with the worn but functional midcentury furniture we had inherited from my grandmother Marion. In my mind, cleanliness was the mark of prosperity. And so, like Richard and Karen, I too endeavored toward perfection, albeit perfection of a different kind, on behalf of my parents and the dreams I thought we shared, in the suburbs that were supposed to furnish them for us.

— 2 —

FOR ALL WE KNOW

Karen spent most of her life in the master-planned splendor of Downey, California. She learned how to keep time playing drums at Downey High, with what would become the Carpenters' characteristic precision. She'd harbored a minor musical crush on a Latino kid in the band, Frankie Chavez, and asked him to teach her how to play after several failed efforts at mastering more ladylike instruments like the flute, the glockenspiel, and the accordion. As Karen recalled in multiple interviews, "All I ever heard was 'girls don't play drums.'" Her new high school band director, Bruce Gifford, insisted, "That's not really normal"—a deeply ironic observation given that Karen's discovery of the drums would inevitably become the gateway to the Carpenters' emergence as the exemplars of pop normalcy.[1]

The rambunctiousness of her New Haven childhood a receding memory, the newly teenaged and exercise-averse Karen also wanted an excuse to get out of gym class, so drumming ensured she would be indispensable to the marching band. When I first read Ray Coleman's *The Carpenters: The Untold Story* a number of years ago,

I fan-fictionalized a more elaborate, amorous relationship between Karen and Frankie the drummer boy, based purely on the line, "she admired the drumming of a young Frankie Chavez." As a recovering SoCal suburban band geek myself, I knew all too well about the hormonal frenzy in public school music practice rooms, especially when drums and drummers were involved. And as a brown, butch lesbian named Karen who worked through a whole hell of a lot of gender trouble in the quasi-militarized structure of marching band, with captains for every section (drums, color guard, and the horn line, for which I was the captain), I could identify with both sides of the Karen/Frankie slash. Sure, I was Karen, but I also wanted to be—I probably already was—Frankie.

In 2009, while I was lollygagging around a friend's backyard in Long Beach, Karen's old college stomping grounds, I went so far as to work up a treatment of a jukebox musical based on the depths of intimacy I imagined between Karen and Frankie, using music from the Carpenters' catalogue, with a couple of originals I crafted with my dad, enlisting his skills (pro bono, of course) as a pianist, composer, and arranger. It would be called *For All We Know*. The show would move back and forth across time from the mid- to late 1970s, at the peak and encroaching decline of the Carpenters' popularity, to Karen's years in high school, foregrounding her budding relationship to the drums, to her musicianship, and to Frankie. These entirely fantastic speculations about her amorous, and also tomboyish, past would hazard an explanation for how and why she could sing so convincingly about love and intimacy, despite the fact that she seemed to experience so little of it in her personal life. *For All We Know* would open with a scene of the Carpenters performing on tour, looking lackadaisical on stage, as if their minds were elsewhere.

> *For All We Know*, SCENE ONE. Karen sings "For All We Know" from behind the drums while her focus drifts off to another place, to a tender reminiscence. The setting shifts around her, as if in a blur, just as the song trickles to an unanticipated stop. We've been transported a decade earlier to the band room at Downey High. Stripped of the Carpenters' side musicians and unexceptional stagecraft, Karen is left standing in the middle of the stage with her snare drum, struggling with her grip. A cocky kid with a demi-pompadour named Frankie comes up to her and teases her about her sticks, like she's Anybodys from *West Side Story* and he's one of the Jets calling out her tomboyish hubris. The teasing abates after his awkward efforts at flirtation become all too apparent. He helps adjust her grip on her sticks. She gets it right.

In her own way, Karen Carpenter also wanted to be Frankie: she wanted to wield the sticks, to set the beat. During Jerry Dunphy's visit to the Carpenters' home, broadcast as "Jerry Dunphy Visits the Carpenters," he asked Karen the question she fielded most during her earliest days in the spotlight, especially from avuncular TV anchors of his ilk: "Karen, one thing that's always been in short supply is pretty girl drummers. How'd this all get started?" In answering this question, she'd usually smirk to herself, or expel a chuckle tinged with more exasperation than amusement, before playfully rolling her eyes and diving into the answer with varying degrees of specificity. Karen did all three things to Jerry before she told him, "When I was in high school, I was influenced by a friend of mine that had been playing drums since he was three years old, and he really knocked me out. So I really liked the drums, and decided to take them up."

Several years later, in a 1976 radio interview with DJ Charlie Tuna on LA's KIIS FM, Karen mentioned her direct inspiration by name: "In my junior year I got real friendly with a kid named Frankie Chavez, who was head of the drum line. . . . I said, 'Let me see if I can play. I know I can play.' I went over, I picked up a pair of sticks. It was the most natural feeling thing I've ever done, and that was it."[2]

For All We Know, SCENE TWO. Karen and Frankie are lingering on the football field after night practice with the marching band. The band director forgot his transistor radio on the drum major's stand, and the two turn it on, sliding through static and snippets of song until they land on something with a strong broadcast signal. It's doo-wop. They lie back on the grass and stare at the stars. Frankie tells her it's his favorite kind of music because it's both tough and romantic. Karen giggle-scoffs at the earnest pretension of that remark. Frankie sings along. Karen listens. The two lean in as if to kiss, but the DJ on the radio interrupts with his slick, booming, rock-jock voice over the song's fade. He kills the mood by playing "Please Mr. Postman." They each turn away as if to shrug off what just happened. Or what didn't happen. The atmosphere lightens. With the swooning spell of doo-wop broken, the two get back to goofing around like the drum-line buddies they are, poking at each other with their sticks.

In an effort to explain why their relationship never evolved beyond the innocuous status of "good buddies," despite the fact that Karen may have been "smitten" (in biographer Randy Schmidt's words), Frankie observed that Karen "had that little tomboy streak to her and used to talk like a beatnik. I loved that she would talk like a jazz player."[3] Karen's musicianship, her adeptness at an instrument—the drums—and her ability to talk like a "player" gave her access to the ensembles of largely male musicians Richard assembled to perform locally shortly after he started attending California State University, Long Beach, in 1964, which was a mere twelve miles south of Downey. Her athleticism from childhood was sublimated into her music and into the earliest expressions of her musicality. She always considered herself a drummer who sang, not the other way around. "It was difficult for her to leave the drums," explains her former college classmate turned band mate, Gary Sims. "She really enjoyed drumming. It was part of her persona."

> *For All We Know*, SCENE THREE. *In a recording studio.* Karen and Richard are covering "Please Mr. Postman" for the 1973 *Now and Then* album. Though everyone assumes Richard is the tyrannical perfectionist who holds session musicians hostage in the studio, we see it's actually Karen calling the shots, interrupting takes because things "aren't quite right." The tempo is too slow, she complains. She bangs her sticks together to prod everyone else into picking things up. She keeps hammering out the pace. It isn't upbeat enough. It doesn't feel right. It should be more fun. It *needs* to be more fun, she insists, punctuating each complaint with another smack of the sticks. She comes up with the idea of doing a retro DJ intro. Something to interrupt the sluggish, ambivalent mood. Richard thinks the DJ shtick is hokey and resists. She demands it. It's best that way. He relents. They resume recording, and she and the rest of the band tackle the chorus with renewed vim and vigor.

There's a photograph of Karen on tour with the Carpenters in 1975 wearing a custom-made iron-on tee with the words LEAD SISTER in block letters across the front. As Richard explained in an online chat with fans, a Japanese magazine had mistakenly translated the word *singer* as *sis-*

ter in an interview with them during their 1974 world tour. Karen thought it was hilarious and had the T-shirt made the following year to wear for a special drum bit in which she soloed, marching band–style, on a snare during the middle of their show. The largest fan organization dedicated exclusively to Karen is called Lead Sister in honor of the iconic images of her wearing that shirt and rocking her snare. The joke behind the term *lead sister* is a cruel one, insofar as it reveals a pointed and painful truth about Karen Carpenter: she was the lead, the star, yet she was defined, both in public and in private, by her relationship to her brother. As biographer Randy Schmidt writes in *Little Girl Blue*, "Richard had long been the musical prodigy, and she was his tagalong."[4]

* * *

Karen herself explained that no one quite knew what to do with her when the family first arrived in Southern California—or ever, really. She imagined herself as a "nurse" or an "artist" in her middle-school autobiography assignment, and ultimately she wasn't too far off with those adolescent projections into the future. Karen was her brother's musical caretaker, always ready with the assist behind the scenes. Yet she was also the one forced out front who would eventually become revered in life and death as the more soulful artist of the two. Karen's voice is the "natural," emotional conduit to her artistry, whereas Richard comes across as studied, passionless, and maybe even conniving. In another segment of "Jerry Dunphy Visits the Carpenters," Karen remarked on her own aimlessness in contrast to Richard's single-minded pursuit of his musical career: "I didn't really have any ideas of where I was going, but he'd always wanted to be exactly where he is. He had ideas, but I didn't know I could do anything until sixteen. And when I took up the drums, both the drums and the voice started to come together."

The Carpenters spent several years settling into Downey, starting in 1963. Karen was thirteen; Richard was sixteen going on seventeen. The family squeezed themselves into tiny, spartan apartments throughout those early years before their house in New Haven sold and they could afford a Southern California home capacious enough to accommodate a real piano for Richard. During those early days in Downey, Agnes and Harold would schlep their son to various auditions and weekend talent competitions at local community venues like Furman Park. Though he never actually won, this local exposure yielded some tangible gains. Richard scored a weekly gig as the accompanist at the Downey Methodist Church, which became a gateway to other area casuals like weddings and gigs at restaurants and bars (even though he was still underage).

Karen did actually tag along wherever her brother went, accommodating his and their parents' requests to support Richard's budding career by whatever means necessary. Her signature contralto still latent and undiscovered, Karen was enlisted to sing for Richard at one of the Furman Park talent contests. The duo was received with no particular fanfare. She was still stuck in her head voice and hadn't quite tapped into the sweet spot of her lower registers—something Dionne Warwick would later describe as the sound of "smoking wood." Karen joined the choir at the church where her brother played piano, but as with most suburban kids conscripted into the innocuous pastimes and side hustles of their older siblings, nothing especially revelatory happened for Karen during this period, at least relating to her musical development. According to Agnes, "She took a little bit longer to take an interest [in music]. She liked baseball first; then she went into drums. Suddenly she wanted drums."[5]

On their TV specials, Richard and Karen built jokey segues around how Karen annoyed her older brother by drumming on any and every household surface right after she first took up the instrument. As Randy Schmidt describes, "At home she assembled the kitchen barstools and even a few pots and pans to simulate a drum kit. Her father's chopsticks served as drumsticks." She played along with jazz records, by artists like the Dave Brubeck Quartet and Buddy Rich's sextet, which came in handy when she and Richard recorded their first demo, including their own rendition of Duke Ellington's classic number "Caravan."

For All We Know, SCENE FOUR. *After school at Frankie's house.* Karen and Frankie are in his room listening to

Buddy Rich records, snacking on donuts and hot dogs, because Frankie swears they're Buddy's favorite foods. Karen chides him for his naïve notion that scarfing a couple of hot dogs and crullers will endow them with the superpower to play as fast and tight as Buddy. There are no drums in the room, just low-lying surfaces of various shapes and sizes: a step stool here, a thick dictionary there, a couple of old Tinkertoy canisters, a pink donut box.

KAREN argues with Frankie about whether a traditional or matched grip is better for stick control. (She prefers traditional.) He doesn't think she can keep up with Buddy, at least at this stage, with that "crummy traditional grip." Frankie turns up the song they've been listening to in the background—the Buddy Rich sextet's recording of "Caravan." With that little bump in the volume, Frankie has dropped the gauntlet.

KAREN and Frankie start playing along, at first trading riffs and rolls back and forth on the unused schoolbooks stacked just in front of them, dueling in a polite, gentlemanly manner with contrasting grips, drumsticks akimbo. By the time the long drum solo commences at minute four, they dispense all decorum and compete for every available surface in the room, using open desk drawers to simulate cymbal rides, elbowing each other out to tap on the mustard jar or a plate of half-eaten hot dogs, knocking books and other heavy items over in time to the music itself, simulating kick drums and the taut staccato of a closed hi-hat. A cacophonous arrhythmia ensues, albeit strangely in time with "Caravan," as each attempts to out-joust the other with fills, rolls, starts, and stops. Just as they summit the peak of this (barely) controlled chaos, the flute seizes the melody, signaling the end of the drum solo on the recording. It comes as a relief to them both. They collapse onto the disheveled aftermath of their exertions, seeming quite pleased with themselves.

Karen's first drum set was purchased in the San Fernando Valley with Frankie in tow. Agnes and Harold enlisted him to come along and help them make the most prudent selection of a kit that would be suitable for Karen's skill level at that time. It didn't take long for Karen to request an upgrade. Having outgrown the marching band snare and her entry-level Ludwig kit, Karen began gigging with Richard on whatever casuals he managed to book, from accompanying community theater musical productions to competing in—and winning—the Hollywood Bowl's amateur Battle of the Bands in 1966, where a sixteen-year-old Karen wowed the judges with her poised and lengthy drum breaks in their mostly jazz-oriented set list.

It took a lot for Richard and the Carpenters' management team to convince Karen to come out from behind the drums to take her proper place, lead singing out front. The change came gradually, as a result of some difficulty finding the right angles to film her from behind for their 1971 television special, *Make Your Own Kind of Music*. At first she agreed to step out front only for the ballads. Once they finally achieved her consent to hire a string of touring drummers later that year, they were left with the problem of figuring out a way to work elements of her drumming back into their stage show. This wasn't simply to appease her discomfort and give her hands something to do—in her own words, "There was nothing to hold on to, nothing to hide behind"; they used these set pieces to remind everyone else—their audiences, their fans—how it all began. Karen was always part of the band, not just its luminous lead singer.

The "lead sister" act I referred to earlier—with Karen trotting onstage in her jeans and custom-made tee to rock a solo snare and other percussion instruments for Richard's Sousa-esque arrangements of Gershwin tunes—is among the most beloved, most documented drum-centric shticks in the Carpenters oeuvre. There were several different iterations of the act, but the one featured on their TV special begins with Richard being introduced first. He launches, with all the Liberace bravado a nice boy like him can muster, into a few baroque flourishes on his piano before settling into a vaudevillian canter. He sings lead on a segue—a novelty number in the spirit of "Piano Picker," their cheeky autobiographical excursus behind the music of the Carpenters:

Learnin' all the latest hit records
From the radio by ear
I was dreamin' I'd be famous

When a big surprise appeared
She was a five-foot-four tornado
A pair of drumsticks in her hand

Just as the "big surprise" of Karen's musical ability interrupts Richard's long-simmering fantasies of fame, the song
modulates momentarily into a minor key. It's at this moment
that Karen careens tornadolike onto the stage, unholsters
her drumsticks and takes the number over with snare fills
for "Strike Up the Band." As was always the case, these
were Richard's arrangements, but they were crafted to let
Karen shine. In his review of the "lead sister" bit for *Modern Drummer*, Rod Fogarty describes the exuberant display
of Karen's prowess: "Karen fills in the spaces like a great tap
dancer, dividing this rudimental workout between the head
and rim of the snare drum. Moving to full drum set, she
sails into some fast swing on the hi-hat, while maintaining
a samba ostinato with her feet."[6]

Sherwin Bash, the band manager from 1970 to 1975,
described what lay beneath the schlocky, good-natured
staging of the duo's sibling rivalry:

> I don't think [Richard] was ever truly happy on the road,
> because once there was an audience, the audience obvi-
> ously loved and adored Karen. There was tremendous
> love and respect between the two of them, but I think
> Richard was jealous. You couldn't go and explain to the
> thousands of people every night who were sitting out

in the audience that "I wrote this. I produced it." What they came and what they saw was, "She's singing it!" He looked like a piano player back there, even though we had lights on him and all that.[7]

The poignant reality beneath all the scripted joviality was that Richard understood it was supposed to be about him privately, in the protective structure of the family. Publicly, however—to the adoring audiences, to the press, to the critics who would enshrine their musical legacy—it would always be about Karen. How could it not be? She was the surprise, the pearl surfacing beautifully formed from the unseen friction and vigorous polishing concealed beneath a protective shell. And so the pathways were set: Karen understood that privately, in the familial realm of love and safety, Richard remained—and would always be—the priority. Richard knew Karen was of the world, and for the world: the figure of sacrifice to stardom. Each protected the very structures most wounding to themselves. For Richard that was the Carpenters, the band, the brand, and its superstar named Karen. For Karen it was the family's ambitions, which were Richard's ambitions.

Comfortably settled into Downey by 1967, Karen followed her brother to Cal State Long Beach, where he was pursuing his dream of becoming a composer and professional musician. By default his dreams were hers, and like their parents, who relocated the family across the country to foster Richard's musical aspirations closer to Hollywood—whether Richard agrees with that version of the story or not—Karen too would continue to pursue the paths carved by her brother's destiny.

— 3 —

LONG BEACH STATE OF MIND

Long Beach was nicknamed "Iowa by the Sea" in the early twentieth century, because it offered a sunny sanctuary for throngs of transplanted midwesterners. Though it was only twenty minutes away by car, Long Beach was a world away from Downey, at least when it came to the Carpenters' musical as well as personal development. Long Beach—specifically Cal State Long Beach—is where the "Spectrum sound," later to be both celebrated and derided as the pristine, obsessively produced Carpenters' sound, was cultivated. Ironically, Richard and Karen achieved their greatest successes with a sound that was named after a failed effort, in collaboration with other college pals, to break into the music business as a choral sextet called Spectrum.

An eclectic assortment of musical artists has come from or been discovered in Long Beach, most notably Snoop Dogg, Melissa Etheridge (who gigged regularly at a lesbian bar called the Que Sera), and Jackson Browne, among countless others. With the exception, perhaps, of Snoop and his Doggfathering of the region's gangsta rap, none have marked the space as indelibly as the Carpenters, nor have any had the city and its civic institutions indelibly mark them as they did the Carpenters.

The city's largest cultural venue on the campus of Cal State Long Beach is named the Richard and Karen Carpenter Performing Arts Center. The edifice was built in 1994 and commissioned in part to brand the Cal State Long Beach music program, known locally for its excellence in the area of vocal and choral music, thanks in no small part to the Carpenters. It also stands in tribute to the fact that the "Spectrum sound" was hatched in the school's choir rooms by a coterie of dorky coeds.

Richard started college in 1964. Karen's drumming chops evolved from the regimentation cultivated by the high school marching band to bona fide swinging on a full kit, accomplished by practicing during off hours with Frankie Chavez and playing along at home ad nauseum to various Dave Brubeck Quartet albums. Karen became the drummer for the Dick Carpenter Trio, rounded out by Wes Jacobs, an upright bassist and jazz tuba player Richard met at Cal State Long Beach. Even with Karen still in high school and Richard in college, the instrumental combo began gigging regularly in such Hedwigian venues as the Jolly Knight Steakhouse in Garden Grove. Karen grew into her preferred role as a "player," drumming, while horn players and singers would occasionally sit in for more elaborate gigs to provide melody and vocals.

If you dive deeply into the Carpenters' beautifully maintained archive of early demo recordings, especially as the

Dick Carpenter Trio, it's clear both Richard and Karen had aspirations to serious jazz musicianship, even if their efforts to step up to standards like "Caravan" rarely transcend a youthfully precocious, par-baked sound. Recorded in the Carpenters' living room in Downey in 1965, when Karen was only fifteen, Richard's arrangement of "Caravan" was, in his own words, deliberately "melodramatic" and "intended to feature each musician, especially Karen who had only been playing the drums for a matter of months."[1] The trio erred on the side of "up-tempo" to an extreme, ratcheting up the beats per second of Ellington's epic orchestral original to a comic, cartoon-mouse speediness.

Even the Buddy Rich sextet's rendition of "Caravan," known for the driving intensity and rapidity of its drum break, seems utterly zen by comparison. What the demo does showcase is Karen's stunning novice ability to stay solidly in the pocket, tethering the more experienced musician, Richard, to something close to swinging, even when his virtuosic enthusiasm threatens to push him over the edge of the beat—even as his arrangement nearly pushes the entire *ensemble* beyond the beat. Her "Caravan" solo is stalwart, though sometimes excessively dependent on drumrolls, particularly on the toms, in a manner that attests to her youth and her marching band training. Karen's efforts on the "Caravan" demo were remarkable enough to draw praise from Rod Fogarty of *Modern Drummer*, who wrote: "After a respectable display of swinging and comping, she launches into a solo that can best be described as an explosion of energy and chops."[2]

When Karen finally matriculated at Cal State Long Beach in 1967, following in her brother's footsteps, both Karen and Richard became more immersed in the musical curriculum on campus, where they joined the university choir directed by Frank Pooler. Karen actually began vocally apprenticing with Pooler before she arrived at college, taking weekend voice lessons with the maestro on Saturday mornings in her final years of high school. Agnes and Harold weren't sure their investment in Karen's vocal training was going to good use. Pooler reassured them she had an "arty . . . natural voice" and warned against over-training it, absolving the family of having to continue with her voice lessons if it was too financially taxing.[3]

Karen's natural voice—"the low one," as she and others were often prone to describing it in interviews—didn't surface until she was well into her late teens, just as the Dick Carpenter Trio began competing in various battles of the bands throughout Southern California. The trio eventually made their television debut, with the home court advantage, at Cal State Long Beach, competing in two episodes of *Your All-American College Show* in 1968. Karen was in her freshman year and one of the newest members of Frank Pooler's university choir.

Footage from their two performances on *Your All-American College Show* is all over YouTube, compiled with varying degrees of length and video quality.[4] In their finale performance, captured in its entirety, the scene opens with host Dennis James welcoming audiences to "the California State College at Long Beach," as coed couples self-consciously writhe in front of the band in their grooviest broadcast-ready finery. Stepping center stage, in front of the dancers, James marvels at "this scene that's typical college Americana. Students dancing to the beat of one of their college's favorite groups." Already victorious from the previous episode, the Dick Carpenter Trio launches into a repeat performance of their rendition of Martha and the Vandellas' "Dancing in the Street."

Dressed a little like the Morton salt girl, in a bright yellow mini-length overcoat with bright yellow culottes and a giant white headband (she wore the same exact outfit, only in another color, for their first appearance on the show), Karen and the rest of the trio tackle an accelerated version of the Marvin Gaye–penned tune, at nearly twice its regular tempo. She sits squarely behind the drums, playing and singing with little hint of exertion. The three start to get a little ahead of the beat as they careen into the first chorus, threatening to unravel, until Richard downshifts ever so slightly with his cheeky piano quote of Michel Legrand's "The Shadow of Your Smile." Eventually, the rhythm section takes its foot off the gas, and nestles briefly into a bossa nova groove.

This mellow respite doesn't last for very long. Richard digs hard into his solo break, fingers flitting furiously across the keys, accelerating faster and faster through breakneck jazz riffs around the circle of fifths. He draws his solo to a close with another abrupt change of tone, a classical interlude with a mock gravitas befitting Bach or Handel, before Jacobs takes his turn, soloing on bass, in anticipation of the last verse. The instrumental solo section is capped by what could be described as Karen's rock goddess drum break, covering every inch of her 1965 Ludwig Super Classic in silver sparkle (which, incidentally, is still on display at the Carpenters Performing Arts Center in Long Beach). The Dick Carpenter Trio was crowned one of two winners of *Your All-American College Show* that night in 1968, taking home a trophy and a $1,500 cash prize, bringing their total winnings to $3,500 for the entire competition. Most of that money was quickly reinvested in recording equipment and other gear upgrades.

By the time of their first small-screen triumph, Karen and Richard had already made several efforts to make it in the music business, not only as the Dick Carpenter Trio, but also with Spectrum, which was cobbled together with classmates from the Cal State Long Beach choir. In the fall of 1967, Karen's first semester at Long Beach, another choir connection, Dan Friberg, helped the Carpenters secure an important link to bass player Joe Osborn, of the notorious "Wrecking Crew," a loose assemblage of studio session hotshots who were originally credited as the Phil Spector Wall of Sound Orchestra. Osborn was the very first person to give the Carpenters a record deal, with his ambitious but dinky Magic Lamp records setup in his garage. Recording

sessions at Magic Lamp began after midnight, or on week-
ends, after Osborn himself would wrap up his numerous
choice session gigs in Hollywood and the Valley.

Through multiple twists of fate, Karen and Richard's
recordings at Magic Lamp would end up being assembled
into the shabby demo, distinguished primarily by Kar-
en's voice, that would eventually find its way to Herb Alpert's vacation hi-fi in the resort town of Lake Arrowhead,
California, ultimately landing the Carpenters a recording
contract with A&M. The demo's circuitous path involved
another Cal State Long Beach classmate, Ed Sulzer, who
worked part time at the Autonetics defense plant, a division
of the same North American Aviation plant in which Agnes
Carpenter also punched her time card. Sulzer handed their
demo over to trumpeter Jack Daugherty, who also worked
at the North American Aviation plant. In turn, Daugherty, who would ultimately become the Carpenters' first
producer at A&M, passed the demo on to John Pisano,
Herb Alpert's guitarist. It was literally through a friend of
a friend of a friend that the Carpenters' demo wound its
way to the "A" of A&M.

Before their fateful "discovery" by Alpert in 1969,
another Cal State Long Beach choir member, composition
student John Bettis, became Richard's songwriting partner. Their director, Frank Pooler, yented them together
in 1966. Pooler thought them both clever, and a little odd,
and thus ideal future collaborators. Bettis would eventually
pen the lyrics for "Goodbye to Love," "Top of the World,"

and "Yesterday Once More," among numerous other Carpenters hits and misses. One of Richard and John's earliest collaborations from 1967 was "Mr. Guder," a mildly anti-establishment number that would eventually make its way onto the 1970 album *Close to You*. Richard and John hastily composed it in an act of impish vengeance after they felt wrongfully dismissed from their summer gig playing at Disneyland as an old-fashioned ragtime duo on Main Street. The entertainment supervisor in question, Vic Guder, who in the words of the song, "reflect[s] the company image" and "maintain[s] the rules to live by," swears the boys' summer contract at Disneyland had simply run out. The two imagined they were being punished for forsaking the approved repertoire of quaint turn-of-the-century numbers, instead taking requests for pop hits by the Beatles and the Doors.[5]

It was Richard's easy, early collaboration with his choirmate Bettis and the mentorship of Frank Pooler in the university choir that prompted his efforts to explore a choral approach to pop with a Romantic and orchestral sensibility. To this end, Richard assembled a vocally driven quintet, then a sextet once Karen arrived at college in 1967. Two other Cal State Long Beach students rounded out the ensemble he put together to execute this sound: Gary Sims, a science major who played rock guitar (he met Richard in the local church choir), and Leslie Johnston, another solo vocalist with a higher range than Karen's "low voice." Johnston actually became the lead vocalist in what they collectively dubbed Spectrum. An important precursor to the Carpenters' own overdubbed vocal sensorium, Spectrum performed choral pop with a harmonic sound akin to that of the Beach Boys, only scored with more elaborate time signatures and jazz syncopations inspired by the Dave Brubeck Quartet, who were all the rage in California at the time.

Listening to the most widely available Spectrum recording to this day, their original number, "All I Can Do"—compiled first on the Carpenters box set *From the Top*, released in 1991, and more recently on the 2002 *The Essential Collection (1965–1997)*—one can discern some distinct precursors to the Carpenters' signature sound, albeit under a more experimental guise. Like the Dick Carpenter Trio's "Caravan," "All I Can Do" was also recorded in the Carpenters' home in Downey with Karen and Richard's two-track Sony 200. In the liner notes to *From the Top*, Richard says the musical accompaniment track for "All I Can Do" was recorded "in the living room on one track," while the vocals were recorded in their bathroom on the remaining track "in a futile attempt at some echo."[6] Spectrum couldn't afford any further studio time at Magic Lamp or at United Audio Recording Studio in nearby Santa Ana, despite Ed Sulzer's enthusiastic management of the group and his knack for booking them gigs around Los Angeles, including a weeklong residency at Ledbetter's in Westwood and an opening turn for Steppenwolf, of all headliners, at a club called the Blue Law.

"All I Can Do" features gender-split unison singing—first the girls, then the boys—across tight minor modulations and syncopated rhythms. Karen and Leslie Johnston blend well on the closest thing to a melody in the song, though Karen's unmistakable timbre remains texturally dominant over Johnston's voice. The other four members of the sextet—all male voices, including Richard's—perform the work of rhythmic transition and tonal modulation throughout. All told, Spectrum sounded like a cross between the type of jazz vocal groups audiences would grow more accustomed to a decade later, like the Manhattan Transfer, and the pop harmony groups they were already used to hearing on the radio, like the Mamas and the Papas, the Association, and the Fifth Dimension.

In fact, with their matching blazers and neatly trimmed bowl cuts, Spectrum came across as a fussier, buttoned-up, art school version of the Fifth Dimension. Despite Spectrum's dramatic play with dynamics and syncopated zigzagging across time signatures, the choral group still managed to sound more square than soulful, whereas an ensemble like the Fifth Dimension achieved a soulfulness, in spite of the squareness of some of the arrangements of their major hits like "Up, Up, and Away." Like Richard and Karen, Marilyn McCoo, one of the Fifth Dimension's founding members (who later became the post–Dionne Warwick host of TV's *Solid Gold*), also had her roots in choir and church singing. Yet the style of choral singing at the core of the Fifth Dimension's ensemble approach couldn't have been more different from Spectrum's.

Gospel choirs and the black church figured prominently in the Fifth Dimension's own choral approach to pop *and* soul. Indeed, many original members of the group, including McCoo, Ronald Towson, and Billy Davis Jr., began singing in gospel choirs, whereas the Carpenters, under the tutelage of Pooler at Cal State Long Beach, were drastically underexposed to gospel, spirituals, and soul during their musical development and training. Even the jazz artists Richard and Karen admired most from childhood onward—Dave Brubeck, Bill Evans, Buddy Rich, and some of the old timers Richard loved listening to from their parents' record collection, like Frankie Laine and Al Jolson—were white. The "sonic color line" described by literary and cultural studies scholar Jennifer Stoever in her book of the same title was in many respects clearly delimited and reflexively observed by the Carpenters, especially during their Spectrum experiments.[7]

It also bears mentioning that their maestro, Frank Pooler, who was otherwise known for being "a bit of a maverick in the choral music world," had a notoriously limited relationship with gospel and spiritual repertoires.[8] Pooler even went so far as to say, "I don't want to do music that's foreign to me," when the subject of black spirituals arose during a conversation about selecting numbers for his a cappella ensemble at the university.[9] Eventually, Pooler shifted his stance with the intervention of African American students like Wendy Freeman, who sang several duets with Karen when they were in the university choir together, and who took the lead in diversifying the Cal State Long Beach repertoire, paving the way for its musical transformation in later decades.[10] Through Freeman's and others' interventions, Pooler became more open to gospel and spirituals, despite skewing more often to his "maverick" comfort zone of avant-garde and experimental numbers in the American art music vein (think lots of Aaron Copland).

The Spectrum sound, then—the seed of the Carpenters' own distinctly bright, some might say saccharine, over-dubbed vocal approach—had its roots in the segregation of "experimental" choral styles, from vernacular styles like gospel and black church music. Pooler aptly describes the sharp, "straight" (i.e., without vibrato) vowel sounds the Carpenters perfected in their recordings and live performances as filtered through "a Disneyland smile."[11]

The most important modifications to the Spectrum sound occurred after the ensemble failed to make a dent in the music scene in the years 1968 and 1969, despite a vigorous show schedule, which included hip Hollywood venues like the Troubadour and Whisky-a-Go-Go. Having downsized once again to a duo with Karen, Richard began to experiment with overdubbing, replicating the harmonically intricate Spectrum sound with their two voices alone: the locus classicus would be "I Won't Last a Day without You," with its orgy of choral interludes and tight, five-part melismatic riffs—a controlled chaos of undulating notes stretched across a single syllable of lyric—until they coalesce into a tidy, harmonic resolution. As biographer Randy Schmidt wrote, "Although the arrangements were identical to those of [their failed vocal sextet] Spectrum, there was something special about the familial sound that resulted from the layering of Karen's voice with Richard's."[12]

This wall of harmony, once a product of the pair's exogamous experiments with choral collaborators from school and church, winnowed itself to what we now recognize as the Carpenters' sound: a seemingly insular one, with a sweet layering that owes its richness to what is in essence an infinite redoubling of sameness. It is a sameness born of the suburbs and nurtured in Southern California's emblematic structures: in its garages, churches, chain family restaurants, and public schools; in the region's many defense plants; in its vacation mountain getaways; at Cal State Long Beach.

Beyond the surf and sand, it is this Southern California, an interconnected sprawl of suburbs with a surfeit of good public schools, venerable places of worship, and reasonably priced theme restaurants with live music from bands like the Dick Carpenter Trio, that seduced so many mid-century dreamers of the golden dream. This is the same fantasy peddled across the Pacific through the Carpenters' cavalcade of hits, and through Karen's welcoming voice in which (like Ella Fitzgerald's) you could always hear the subtle curve of a smile, even if she was singing about tears.

At the height of the duo's success, their old choir director, Frank Pooler, wrote a specialized analysis of "The Choral Sound of the Carpenters" in 1973 for *The Choral Journal*. Referring perhaps to their earlier efforts with Spectrum, Pooler writes: "The original Carpenters are highly skilled choral singers and were selected by Richard Carpenter for that reason. Their vocal ensemble sound is based on absolute vowel uniformity and a frontally focused brilliant 'ē' vowel."[13] He praises their breath control and the group's workarounds for troublesome diphthongs (double vowel sounds, like the *oy* in *boy*), echoing other accounts of their precision and perfectionism, both live and in the studio. At the end of his piece, Pooler predicts that the Carpenters' choral influence in pop will "rapidly expand" thanks to the role music educators played in "securing Carpenter concerts for their localities."

*   *   *

Rick Woodbury, my high school choir director at Ramona High School in Riverside, California (about sixty miles northeast of Long Beach), also happened to be an alumnus of Frank Pooler's Carpenters-era Cal State Long Beach choir. Peppered among his strained efforts at getting us to shut up long enough to rehearse "O Magnum Mysterium" or a *Les Misérables* medley were anecdotes about how Karen used to sit in the tenor section with him in the university choir in the late 1960s. He would flamboyantly re-enact his jaw dropping at the gender trouble Karen, a lyric tenor at times, stirred with her "low voice," then go on to wax nostalgically, and instructively, about the mythical quality of her range. Mr. Woodbury's story-telling would intensify whenever we rehearsed our choral arrangement of "Merry Christmas, Darling," the song for which Pooler wrote the lyrics when he was only eighteen, before he gave up on the melody and hoarded the words for future inspiration. Decades later, he handed the lyrics over to his star pupil, Richard, and within a matter of fifteen minutes, the Carpenters' only original Christmas standard was born.

Mr. Woodbury was the person from whom I first learned that Karen preferred to be known as a drummer and not a singer. I didn't join the choir or the elite audition-only Madrigals vocal ensemble at Ramona High School until the end of my junior year, in spring 1990, even though I (like Karen) joined the marching band right away my freshman year, which totally covered most of my own PE requirements. I never thought I could sing, because I didn't think I was pretty enough and my voice felt too low. Those two failings, at least in my fragile teen psyche, kept my face pressed up against the glass of the choir room (which shared an adjoining set of practice rooms with the marching band), even though deep within my soul, and at the seat of my diaphragm, I desperately wanted—needed—to sing. Until my junior year, I emoted the only way I knew how: by wailing melodiously on the alto saxophone, which for the most part was well received in the late 1980s and early 1990s, the era of peak saxophone.

Harmonies of all varieties always gave me the tingles, and to this day, my wife, Sarah, accuses me of "wantonly harmonizing" whenever we're at karaoke or singing along to the radio in the car. For me, building chord structures with horns and other musical instruments could only approximate the thrill of forging harmonies with just your body—your breath, your upper palate, your uvula, your "mask." I suppose in a high school band there's a degree of imprecision to the tonalities achieved by instruments wielded by teens, so that may have accounted for my preference. To be sure, not all of our vocals in the choir locked perfectly in tune with each other at that age either. They certainly failed the exacting standards of a finely honed Carpenters recording. It just felt different striving to hit the mark with other voices, using vibrations emanating from your own body without the aid of a button, a conduit, or even a sturdy embouchure. Vocal harmony felt like magic. Like you were getting away with a trick. Like you were making meaning, whether it was through a wide-open "ahhhhh" or a bright Disneyland smile.

As an only child who'd spent lots of time on the road with my parents, I always wanted a younger sibling to play with, and I didn't make friends very easily, or for very long, until my days as a touring lounge mouse through the leisure circuit of Southeast Asia ended. We finally landed in the suburbs of Southern California in 1983. During those years on the road, the internationally beloved *Sound of Music* fomented one of my deepest fantasies: a readymade family chorale on hand to perform six- to eight-part harmonies of cherished folk numbers or elaborate, impromptu puppet shows about lonely goatherds and beer-swilling Alpine villagers.

The Von Trapps also made me miss my own musical family in Manila: the late-night sing-alongs and jam sessions interstitially punctuated by breaks for barbecued meats or salty snacks dipped in spiced vinegar. On the road, it was just my parents and me, often living at an opulent resort, where I plumped up on room service as they gigged all night or waited to eat with them and their two backing musicians at the hotel restaurant after closing time.

Far from the enriching din of Manila, or the bleary-eyed glamor of late nights on the road with my folks, the Carpenters stoked my fantasies of another possibility for deep resonance amidst the lonely cul-de-sacs of suburbia: finding harmony with, essentially, oneself. Though the technology of overdubbing eluded me in my early adolescence, its principles, its manufactured warmth, and the mere fact of its multiplying possibility nurtured a young, isolated soul in search of connection.

— 4 —

GOODBYE TO LOVE

Maria Katindig-Dykes and her husband, Jimmie Dykes, had finished a six-month stint at the Hyatt Regency in Singapore and were about to wrap up a six-month residency at the Playboy Jazz Club at Silahis International Hotel in Manila when a telegram appeared under the door early one morning in our Manila suite. It was for Jimmie: MOTHER ILL. CALL HOME. It was sent by his older brother Lee.

My dad called home to find out that his mother, Marion Dykes—the woman who sternly scattered the kids taunting me on the lawn during my first visit to Riverside, California; the woman who plied me with my very first taste of stewed tomatoes—was dying of brain cancer. It was late January 1983, and we made our preparations to leave Manila, unsure of whether or not we would return right away, or ever. I remember turning to my mom on one of the first nights we were in Riverside and asking her in Tagalog if we were ever going back home. She said she didn't know, and we both cried quietly so as not to interrupt the other more urgent processes of loss and mourning happening under the same roof.

By the time the woman I called Lola Marion died a few weeks later—*Lola* is a Tagalog honorific meaning "grandmother"—it became clear that we were in Riverside, California, to stay, at least for a little bit. My parents had never owned a home, and they now stood to inherit part of one. They eventually bought out my Uncle Lee for the whole thing: a three-bedroom midcentury ranch-style in a subdivision akin to the cookie-cutter domiciles in *Back to the Future*. I hadn't really gone to school since the second grade, and I was about to turn ten. There were always vague discussions of settling down somewhere, of "getting established," but we never knew where or when. The occasion of Lola Marion's death seemed the opportune time to try to make good on some of these goals after a nomadic gig-to-gig, resort-to-resort, feast-or-famine existence across the Pacific Rim.

I didn't realize that my affinity for the Carpenters was what they used to call "corny" until I landed in these Southern California suburbs a decade after the Carpenters' heyday and a month after Karen died in Downey in 1983. We were in search of the kind of American prosperity epitomized by a perfectly edged lawn. Or maybe even the proverbial white picket fence. While the other kids in our Riverside, California, subdivision were all abuzz about the latest videos on MTV, my family and I were still very much of another place, out of step with both New Wave (what all the cool kids were listening to at the time) and the newness of most things in America. Despite not having any friends yet in this alien landscape of gleaming appliances and tidy tract homes with concrete driveways, I was thrilled about the prospect of settling down in a place where I could actually ride the bicycle we had carted around, disassembled, in a box to the hotels across southeast Asia where my parents had long-term engagements.

"Karen stayed so basic," the Carpenters' close friend Carol Curb remarked in a 2007 BBC documentary, *Only Yesterday: The Carpenters' Story*: "She wanted the white picket fence. She just wanted to get married. Have children. Be cooking Thanksgiving dinners. And that was her real goal in life." Not unlike my namesake, I was road weary and became increasingly insistent on some kind of normalcy. But also (like Karen), I fundamentally understood that these fantasies of suburban tranquility would always evade me, because I would never really be normal—not because of any gift, or burden, from my own talent, but because such exemplary normalcy is inherently impossible to achieve, let alone maintain, for someone as brown and queer as me, even if I didn't understand that fully then.

The Carpenters' song catalogue bears out these lessons. For each time we feel buoyant with the propitious notion that "We've Only Just Begun," we are bound to struggle with the blues through "Rainy Days and Mondays." For every moment we might feel on "Top of the World," we are also compelled to question why we go on "Hurting Each Other." All of these songs are jarringly different, at least emotionally, and are in close proximity to one another on the Carpenters' most successful albums. And in between these highest highs and lowest lows are detours into the minutiae of other feelings: indifference, novelty, absurdity, benign self-reflection, and a deep nostalgia keyed to forgetting the present in favor of a seemingly simpler, more cherished past.

Most of what I learned very early in my life about love, desire, and the way things are supposed to be came from pop songs and television. I suppose this is true of nearly everyone raised by American pop culture, in whatever part of the world they happen to have encountered it for the first time. For me this mediated relationship to something called "America" felt particularly acute as we bounced between cultures and ways of living, either communally or in a nuclear family unit. The vestiges of empire were redolent in all of the places we lived for any length of time before we landed in Southern California, another contested ground of occupation and imperial conflict buried beneath gleaming stucco monuments to convenience.

For example, I struck up a flirtation with the British Empire in 1982, a year before we arrived in a sunny landscape of missions repurposed as inns and Mexican drivethroughs. I became a precocious eight-year-old Anglophile during my parents' six-month residency in the island nation of Singapore, the place where I was first exposed to British accents, Union Jacks, the Beatles, and Falklands Crisis–era Thatcherism. A former trading post of the British East India Company from the early nineteenth century onward,

Singapore remained under British rule until it was occupied by another aspiring empire, Japan, in World War II. The island city-state eventually gained its sovereignty in 1965, twenty years after the British had resumed control of its territories after the war.

It turns out that when she was a child, my mom also lived in Singapore during its embryonic nationhood in the mid-1960s, while my grandfather had a yearlong musical engagement of his own in the Lion City. I'm convinced my mother's crush on the dreamy, accented Davy Jones of the Monkees had everything to do with her own postcolonial fling with Anglophilia and Union Jacks before she cozied up to the Carpenters and eventually had me.

In 1982 my parents had a plum nightly gig at a 1920s and '30s deco-themed supper club called Nutmeg's at the Hyatt Regency, where they were tasked with playing only jazz standards. For this gig they had to attire themselves in variations on black and white, like they were bringing old movies to life. They occasionally sent a sitter for me through hotel housekeeping, often gruff older women of Chinese heritage who would have none of my monkeying around. When it was established that I couldn't get into too much trouble alone in a hotel room beyond the occasional room service indulgence, I spent most evenings without supervision reading C. S. Lewis books, or watching American miniseries starring Sam Elliott on TV. When my parents finished performing for the night, we'd have a late dinner at the restaurant in the lobby before reclining in the room together and watching the black-and-white Charlie Chan and Sherlock Holmes movies that were broadcast on Singaporean TV well after midnight.

Richard Carpenter shared my family's late-night television habits. Some of the most quintessential songs in the Carpenters' oeuvre were inspired by Richard's own wind-down routine of watching TV in the wee hours after gigs or marathon recording sessions. By now every Carpenters fan, and most pop music aficionados, know that "We've Only Just Begun" was originally just a one-minute jingle written by Roger Nichols and Paul Williams for a Crocker Bank commercial, titled "Wedding." Richard caught the schmaltzy, vaguely cinematic ad, with its solar flare piercing through Vaseline lenses, on TV one night after a late studio session. He recognized Paul Williams's voice on the track, so he called him immediately. The rest, as they say, is history.[1]

It makes perfect sense that "We've Only Just Begun," essentially an ad for how to mortgage one's way into the American dream, became the Carpenters' follow-up single to "Close to You." First comes love, then comes marriage, as they say. Karen's phrasing—unfurling the notion that "we've only just begun to live" in a single breath—is remarkable. The slightest fry in her voice after her first exhalation stretches all the way to "live" and recurs when she finally lands on "promises" in the next phrase, as if she's fatigued from the exertion required by such breathless beginnings. Her phrasing was more natural than breaking up the first line into two, which is what Paul Williams did in the jingle. Karen's style of vocal delivery, with those organic cracks of emotion (or maybe it was simply exhaustion?), offers a sense of why so many singers, musicians, producers, fans, and casual listeners interpret her voice as sad and melancholic. One of Karen's biggest fans, k. d. lang, whose own vocal style was influenced profoundly by her idol, admired Karen because "she sang real simple, with no tricks."[2] Paul Williams, the song's lyricist, had another take: "She had the sound of a bride when she sang ['We've Only Just Begun'], so it's innocent and sensual at the same time."[3]

Sounding like a bride when she sang "We've Only Just Begun" was the closest Karen would come to achieving that "basic" desire her old friend Carol Curb insisted she harbored for a white picket fence, marriage, and kids. Karen made a stab at it a decade later, when she was briefly married to, of all people, a property developer named Tom Burris from 1980 to 1981. (Property developers in Southern California were the early 1980s equivalent of snake oil salesmen in the 1880s Wild West.) Burris ended up fulfilling Karen and her family's worst nightmares, sucking her dry of vast sums of money for the sake of a "flash" lifestyle instead of the simple dreams fostered by that old Crocker Bank ad; a dream that was sold and spread throughout the world by the Carpenters' iconic hit anticipating so much of life ahead and room to grow. "We've Only Just Begun," in short, was a wedding song—*the* wedding song—for a generation and more.

On the other end of the romantic spectrum, "Goodbye to Love"—the first Carpenters' hit cowritten by Richard and John Bettis—also owes its existence to Richard's nocturnal viewing habits. He was watching an old Bing Crosby film on TV called *Rhythm on the River* (1940), in which Crosby and Mary Martin play a pair of musical ghostwriters for a pompous, more successful but creatively blocked scribe played by Basil Rathbone. As Richard explains in the BBC documentary *Only Yesterday*, "Rathbone's most famous song is called 'Goodbye to Love.' You never hear it, they just refer to it." The title inspired Richard to write the first unmistakable bars, with a minor turn at the end of the phrase and the opening lyrics, "I'll say goodbye to love; no one ever cared if I should live or die." Unable to make more progress with the words, Richard ultimately turned to Bettis, his old Long Beach choir pal and anti-Guder co-conspirator, for help with the rest.

Given its origins as a spectral song title in a movie from the 1940s, which was set partly in the 1930s, "Goodbye to Love" could have easily ended up becoming a Carpenters period piece, something on the novelty end of their catalogue. Instead, it is arguably one of their most innovative—if not *the* most innovative—original song in their oeuvre. Some critics and musicians, including Richard himself and the Carpenters' longtime guitarist, Tony Peluso, argue that "Goodbye to Love" is the first true specimen of that subgenre beloved by karaoke enthusiasts—the power ballad—because it was the first middle-of-the-road pop ballad to feature a distorted rock guitar solo.

At the time of the release of "Goodbye to Love" in 1972, the phrase *soft rock* hadn't quite cemented its status as a radio format, though the term was bandied about as a contrast to "hard rock" as early as 1969. In that era soft rock described mellow, acoustically oriented pop in the singer-songwriter idiom and a mix of easy listening that the recording industry categorized as "adult contemporary" based on its chart popularity with a more mature audience than the teens of both genders whose rebelliousness and libidinous energies fueled rock and roll's rise.[4] Bread, Carole King, and James Taylor were among adult contemporary's luminaries in the late 1960s and early 1970s, though the Carpenters eventually came to dominate the format during their heyday in the early to mid-1970s, along with perennials like Barbra Streisand and, eventually, Barry Manilow.

Even though soft rock was in many respects a backdated term that arose to differentiate a wider range of melodic pop from the brusque intensity of hard rock (and is thus not considered a genre of its own), the Carpenters' "Goodbye to Love" crystallized the style in 1972 and portended the ubiquity of the power ballad on soft rock radio in the late 1970s and early 1980s. Andy Zax, a producer and music historian, described soft rock as "more a construct than a genre" in a recent social media discussion.[5] He added: "Certainly, there are examples of ballads with fuzz prior to 'Goodbye to Love' on records by people like the Association et al., but I think 'Goodbye to Love' codifies a particular set of sounds, and it makes sense to use it as a starting point." Though bands like Bread and the Association incorporated rock guitar elements with strings and even choral arrangements on some of their pop ballads like "Make It with You," and "The Time It Is Today," none of their guitar solos *shredded* quite like Tony Peluso's in "Goodbye to Love."

On nearly every Carpenters documentary, and in most of the biographies and music criticism about Karen and the band, Richard makes a powerful bid for "Goodbye to Love" as a watershed moment in the genealogy of soft rock for its unexpectedly stark contrast in style. As the Carpenters' guitarist, Peluso created the memorable, distorted intrusion upon the smoothness of Karen's voice and its typically tranquil musical settings; he makes the bold claim that his solo "changed all" that the Carpenters—and soft rock—represented up until that point.[6] It was Richard who requested the contrasting element of "fuzz guitar," the fly in the ointment of their otherwise familiar, tender approach to pop laced with oboes and solo piano.

Karen was the one who had made the phone call to Peluso, asking him to play guitar for the track. Peluso was in "disbelief" when she rang, and as he recalls, "I played something that was very soft and easy, I tried to stay out of the way. Obviously, it didn't happen. Richard said: 'No, no, no, not like that. Play the melody for five bars and then burn it up! Soar off into the stratosphere. Go for it!' He wanted an aggressive, sawtooth guitar solo in the middle of this Doris Day easy-listening-style record. I thought, 'He can't be serious.'"[7] Richard was.

Peluso continues, "Inadvertently, Richard had broken new ground. No one had ever really mixed the elements of rock 'n' roll and easy listening. Totally crazy. I take a tiny bit of credit for being there and playing it, but it was Richard's great idea. From then on, it became very commonplace for a big power ballad to have a raging guitar solo."[8] While Peluso's bold claim to firstness might be debatable, what's clear is that "Goodbye to Love" elicited a double take of the Carpenters and their music from that moment on, disturbing some of their older fans who were concerned they'd gone over to the dark side. (Their follow-up single, "Top of the World," swiftly quieted these concerns.)

Karen cold opens "Goodbye to Love" with just her voice before the piano accompaniment joins her. As each layer of instrumentation introduces itself in the opening verse— that signature oboe swooping in from above, escorted by a few more anodyne woodwind familiars—Karen has effectively established the vocal pose of a languid and jaded chanteuse.[9] A torch singer of this ilk would be at home crooning in the 1930s-era music scene depicted by *Rhythm on the River*, the source of the song's inspiration, or even headlining at Nutmeg's, the supper club where my mom sang in Singapore.

Were it not for the persistence of a pretty typical pop ballad drumbeat beneath the ostentatious harp flourishes and romantic strings, "Goodbye to Love" could be construed as a successful period piece, recreating the mood of '30s-era torch balladry. That is, until minute 1:24, when the gooey harmonies fade to make way for Peluso's fuzz guitar solo. It's relatively innocuous at first, at least to a contemporary ear reared on Heart, Journey, Survivor, and the countless others who made hard guitars weep with soft sentiments. Peluso's solo begins by echoing the melody without very much shredding until about five bars in, when he starts to take some liberties. Just as swiftly, Karen's voice completes the verse, returning with the gentle response to Peluso's distorted instrumental call, forging an incongruous duet. Beauty meets the Beast. A voice evocative of the past crosses paths with a machine careening into the future (a "mystery to us all")—or at least insisting on an alternate present.

"Goodbye to Love" always struck me as the quintessential Carpenters song for this reason, with its yearning fashioned from genres of the past, yet striving to make its mark on a future—on their *now*. Square and serene as their music is often perceived to be, it endures precisely because of the tumult at its heart, as the gnarled, saw-toothed guitar of "Goodbye to Love" explicitly sounds out for us. Influence and innovation perpetually tug against one another in the Carpenters' music, warring to achieve timelessness, artistry. Karen and Richard bore strong attachments to music from the past but hoped to transpose those influences from the old records in their parents' basement, and the old movies on late-night television, into something contemporary, something that would affirm their inventiveness in perpetuity. "Goodbye to Love" became the Carpenters' first bona fide original hit—their first top-ten single that wasn't an arrangement of someone else's song. It reached number seven on the *Billboard* Hot 100 in June 1972.

It was the first song to call me back to the Carpenters over a decade later, when I too was caught between the past and the mystery of my future. My musical tastes were still developing, sourced entirely from influence and not yet stoked by the siren call of contemporaneity or sharpened by the edge of innovation. The first concert my parents took me to in the United States was Ella Fitzgerald and Joe Pass at the Claremont Colleges in the fall of 1983. I enjoyed it but knew enough not to let the family jazz tradition subsume me, when what I wanted was some connection to pop, to the kids my age who were playing the Journey *Escape* Atari game, which had something to do with a band with the same name (so I gathered).

Journey's "Open Arms" was always on the radio—at least the radios I overheard in our neighborhood—and the soft, tinkling piano and big feelings intensified by growling guitars reassured me I could handle the *now*, especially because it so closely resembled my *then* and *there*: my family's carport in Manila where everyone who was playing mahjong with my grandmother would sing along and mildly rock out to Tony Peluso's solo on "Goodbye to Love."

By 1984 I discovered that the *Parade* magazine that always came with the Sunday paper boasted a special offer, a gateway to musical proficiency even a broke immigrant child without an allowance could afford: the Columbia House record club would send me ten albums for just a penny! I promptly taped Mr. Lincoln's copper visage to the business reply mail card to order Journey's *Escape* and Air Supply's *Greatest Hits* with the new bonus song, "Making Love Out of Nothing at All." (They were all the rage when we lived in Singapore, and I knew almost all of their songs, so it seemed like a safe bet.) Even though I knew it would constitute *two* selections instead of just one, thus winnowing my other potential pathways to musical popularity with my peers, I also made sure to nab a copy of the Carpenters' double-album collection of hits, *Yesterday Once More*. "Goodbye to Love" was the last track on side one, just after their cover of "Ticket to Ride," which I'd never heard before.

I invited the January brothers, Ricky and Randy, two ginger-haired boys from next door, roughly around my age, to come over and listen to my new records as soon as I got them in the mail. After scarfing *Escape* nose to tail and pumping power fists in unison to its closer, "Open Arms," I was certain the next appropriate item on our listening agenda would be the Carpenters' classic "Goodbye to Love." Given that I was a total tomboy like Karen—I played soccer with the Januarys on our adjoining lawns—and given that we were collectively too innocent and dorky to find power ballads tingly and romantic, the thought hadn't crossed my mind that I was setting up a playlist of what could otherwise be characterized as "slow-dance songs."

I dropped the needle on "Goodbye to Love." Both Ricky and the slightly younger, maybe even more susceptible Randy immediately hated it. My concerted efforts at making myself seem somehow less foreign and strange were unraveling with each bar, with each embellishment of overdubbed choral backing vocals. It felt out of time and out of place, reminding me without a doubt that so was I. They laughed, groaned, and called it a day, and though they didn't use the word *corny*, I knew that's what they were thinking. That was one of the few words I'd heard before to describe such excesses of sentiment, like the schlock and awe of Peluso's rugged guitar getting mixxy with Karen's plaintive if also always placid voice. *Cheesy* hadn't yet achieved its ubiquity to account for the same shame-inducing attachment to things that seemed incongruous with their moment.

Corny is a word that retains its saliency in everyday usage in the Philippines, even though it has long been phased out of the American vernacular. The fact that I kept using it, then, if primarily to punish myself for my failed efforts at assimilation by touting my affection for decades-old soft rock, says something about how out of synch I truly was when I first landed in SoCal's neatly planned subdivisions where newer meant better.

To be corny is to be "mawkishly old-fashioned; tiresomely simple and sentimental," and this definition describes my attachment to the Carpenters with searing precision. Even though Karen was supposed to be my gateway to a whole new world, albeit a world obsessed with yesterdays once more, she actually ended up being the anchor to my old one: to the Philippines, where *corny* still means something. And even if the Carpenters were perceived to be the whitest of musical acts—even by the ginger-headed January brothers—and engineered in the most white bread of contexts, nothing felt more Filipino to me in those first lonely years fresh off the boat than the sound of Karen's voice.

Decades later, the lead singer of Four Non Blondes and smash hit composer, Linda Perry, reflected, "I feel that there was something bigger . . . We will probably never know what was going on, because [Karen's] voice had too much soul, too much heartbreak, too much pain in it to be just an insecurity."[10] Like my namesake, I felt lost in the eternal sunshine of Southern California, adrift in something bigger than the insecurity its prevailing message of joy and the good life inspired in disoriented souls. Both of us were longing without knowing exactly what for.

– 5 –

QUEER HORIZON

At the height of her fame, Karen's distorted physical self-image worsened when she was confronted with her own figure everywhere: on album covers, in magazines and newspapers, and on television. Add to that the unyielding work ethic their middle-class parents indoctrinated them with, and inevitably the pressure became impossible to conceal even beneath the Carpenters' unperturbed veneer. Karen had to be hospitalized for exhaustion and malnutrition in 1975 due to a punishing work schedule compounded by her secret struggle with anorexia nervosa.

At that high point in their careers, the dogged perfectionism the Carpenters modeled in their recording practice saturated whatever interstitial moments remained of their everyday lives. In 1975, shortly after they had to cancel their lucrative fall overseas tour because of her undisclosed "illness," Karen admitted in an interview with Ray Coleman for *Melody Maker*: "Richard and I have never had a vacation. And it's stupid for the two of us to let it get carried to that amount of work and it turned out to be harmful for me. It's going to be a whole learning process for me to do things in a different way [and] to really seriously calm down and do things at a slower pace, because I'm very regimented. . . . I go to bed at night with a pad by the bed and the minute I lie down it's the only quiet time of the day. My mind starts going: 'This has gotta be done, that's gotta be done, you've gotta call this.'"[1]

This forced interruption due to Karen's physical collapse after unrelenting road and recording schedules also marked the start of a precipitous decline in the Carpenters' chart dominance from the first half of the 1970s.

By the end of 1975, the Carpenters were on the waning side of what Neil Tennant of the Pet Shop Boys cannily described as an act's "imperial phase," or a performer's commercial and cultural peak.[2] From 1970 to 1975, the Carpenters logged twelve top-ten hits, including three number-one and five number-two singles, for a total of fourteen gold records. Even their lowest-charting hit of that era lingered on the cusp of the top ten at number twelve, 1972's "It's Going to Take Some Time."

After 1975 only one of their songs would reach the *Billboard* top twenty, let alone approach the top ten: their cover of Herman's Hermits' "There's a Kind of Hush" peaked at number twelve in 1976. None of their releases after that would even come close. Their 1975 album *Horizon*, with covers of the Eagles' "Desperado" and Neil Sedaka's "Solitaire," and original hits like "Only Yesterday," was their first LP to fall short of multiplatinum status, even though it was widely praised by critics for being their most sophisticated album to date. The duo took advantage of recent studio upgrades at A&M to even further perfect their pristine sound, with brand-new twenty-four-track decks and 30 Dolby. While their follow-up, *A Kind of Hush* (1976), also ultimately went gold, their subsequent albums failed to make much of an impact on the Hot 100, though the duo continued to make strong showings on the easy listening and adult contemporary charts through 1977.

Popularity waxes and wanes, and five years of chart dominance is certainly nothing to sneeze at. But as music critic Tom Ewing reminds us about imperial phases, "There's something double-edged about the concept: It holds a mix of world-conquering swagger and inevitable obsolescence."[3] Perhaps, then, this is why the Carpenters began to undertake a concerted effort to redefine their public image, reframing the terms of their very own normalcy not as "exemplary," or even a lifestyle to be aspired to, but as a license to be "flawed" instead. Karen and Richard both felt their straitlaced image prevented the rock cognoscenti from taking them seriously as musicians.

"The fact that we took a shower every day was swooped on as symbolic," Karen complained to Ray Coleman in their *Melody Maker* conversation. "In an interview once, somebody asked Richard if he believed in pre-marital sex and he said yes, and the woman wouldn't print it! We were labeled as don't-do-anything!"[4] Karen went on to insist she would smoke if she actually liked it, and that the two were "very into wine" even though they weren't "lushes or anything."

As people, Karen wanted to make it clear that she and her brother were far from perfect, despite their fastidious hygiene. As musicians, however, she wanted it to be known that she and Richard would never relinquish their quest for perfection: "Our life is our music, creating it. We try to do everything with as much perfection as we can."[5] Karen began to lay the groundwork of excuses for why both she and her brother, who was struggling with addiction to quaaludes in the mid-1970s, might not live up to all the impossible expectations they established for their music, and that others established for their pop personae.

The moody, soft-focused album cover for 1975's *Horizon*—the zenith of their critical success—says it all: the Carpenters name and logo, featured prominently on the five albums leading up to it, is nowhere to be found. They were no longer in need of any introduction or contextualization. It was just Karen and Richard standing together, alone, looking serious and remote. Karen's pose is plaintive, distracted, and vaguely seductive, her eyes downcast and averted from the camera. Richard stares directly into it, chest open, hands in his back pockets, in a power pose of imperial swagger and defiance.

* * *

Nearly every Carpenters biography, documentary, made-for-TV movie, and lurid tabloid news magazine in print or on television has insinuated, if not overtly advanced, the thesis that Karen Carpenter's anorexia nervosa was triggered by a dearth of affection and love from her mother, Agnes. Randy Schmidt, the author of the authoritative biography *Little Girl Blue: The Life of Karen Carpenter*, describes Agnes's "hypnotic hold" on her daughter, which included interfering in Karen's love life as well as with her professional choices.[6]

After a brief spell living in Beverly Hills in 1975 with her boyfriend Terry Ellis (who also happened to be the founder of Chrysalis records), Karen absconded to the family home in Downey while he was out of town on business. For his part, Ellis speculates that Karen bowed to the maternal pressure that had always placed Richard at the center of the Carpenters' cosmology: "At a very early age, Karen was told that her job in life was to support Richard. That continued all the way up through their careers until they became huge stars and beyond. If you go into the family environment where I was a lot, there was that same dynamic of 'Everybody's here for Richard.' . . . Even when Karen had become the star, that dynamic still existed, and she would fall in line."[7]

The Emmy Award–winning variety show producer Bob Henry, who directed the 1977 TV special *The Carpenters at Christmas*, remembers that he approached Agnes after the broadcast to praise Karen's charming performance. Agnes abruptly interrupted Henry's encomium for Karen to say, "Wasn't Richard wonderful?!?"[8] A mountain of anecdotal evidence like this, compiled by Randy Schmidt, Ray Coleman, and other Carpenters biographers confirms the lifelong tension between Karen and her controlling mother, who only sparingly offered morsels of approval, even at the peak of Karen's popularity. Rob Hoerburger said it most succinctly, when he wrote in the *New York Times* magazine, "If anorexia has classically been defined as a young woman's struggle for control, then Karen was a prime candidate, for the two things she valued most in the world—her voice and her mother's love—were exclusively the property of Richard."[9]

Certainly other factors fueled Karen's anorexia, including her discomfort with moving from behind the drums to the front of the stage to sing. "We had four or five gold records . . . before I finally had to get up [from behind the drums]. Petrified. You have no idea. The *fear*! There was nothing to hold on to," Karen confessed in a 1976 radio interview.[10] Her biographers are also careful to note the dramatic difference between her carefree, tomboyish youth, when she talked like a player—like "one of the boys in the band"—and the period after adolescence, when she first began to notice, and ultimately develop an aversion to, her perceived chubbiness, especially as her voice drew her more attention and physical scrutiny.

I have to admit I never quite understood how so many of the many men who were on Karen's "team" throughout her professional life could have ever described her as a "stocky tomboy prior to 1974."[11] The archival video footage and countless candid and promotional photographs from that era attest otherwise, at least in the eyes of *this* legitimately stocky self-identified tomboy with thick thighs, broad shoulders, and an ample torso. Karen wasn't very tall. In fact, we're the same height (5' 4"). Images of a full-bodied Karen were captured in her mid-teen years, but even then she seemed of average size, if not smaller in relation to the other girls and boys pictured alongside her in choir and band photos. I doubt she would've elicited any comparisons with a linebacker, or with a tank, as I used to when I played in the Riverside girls' softball league as an adolescent.

While it's difficult to deny the numerous accounts of the Carpenters' family psychodramas—of the maternal neglect and sibling rivalry that are widely acknowledged to have aggravated Karen's eating disorder and hastened her death—I'm prone to speculate about a number of other reasons for her hyper-attentiveness to her physicality that may or may not have any basis in what actually happened in her intimate life.

In many respects Agnes is too easy a target in the tragic scenario of Karen's early death. There's something odious about how quick we all are to capitulate to yet another story that casts women as both victim and perpetrator in their dynamic. It keeps all the men in Karen's life and career off the hook as they preserve their roles as mentors, protectors, lovers, friends, brothers. They just couldn't get through to her, they just couldn't get close to her, they all say.

In the postmortem on Karen's life, Agnes has emerged as a type: the suffocating, overprotective mother who arrests her daughter's erotic and social development by keeping her entombed in the family home. When she wasn't on tour, stories abound of Karen being sequestered in Downey like a latter-day Lady of Shalott, or like Rapunzel locked in her tower with Agnes as the witchy sentry. She finally managed to move out of the house for a lengthy spell in July 1975, when she took up residence in Century City's "twin towers" on the Avenue of the Stars. She delighted in decorating her snazzy cosmopolitan condos (two units combined) with her eclectic style that ranged from art deco to French country to adolescent dreamer. Karen famously kept a bed filled with a display of the stuffed animals she received from fans.

Around 1974, when Karen lost considerable weight and began to wear more revealing, backless ensembles, her team expressed concern about her exposure—not so much in a sexual manner, but because her thinness began to elicit concerned gasps from the Carpenters' live audiences. Things had deteriorated to such an extent that the Karen Carpenter fan organization, Lead Sister, had to dispel rumors that she was fighting cancer in their October 1975 newsletter: "Contrary to unfounded reports you may have read in various magazines, please be assured there is no truth in the rumor that Karen is a victim of cancer."[12]

Up until then, and also throughout this crisis of concealment, the layers of familial protection were mimicked in Karen's performance wardrobe. Encased as she so often was in neck-high, floor-length Victorian frocks, or "granny dresses," as she called them, Karen nevertheless became the object of attention, affection, and obsession for many (mostly) male fans. Some even stalked her at the family home, prompting new protocols and security efforts. As she lost more weight, the granny dresses served another purpose: to conceal her protruding bones as she dropped to eighty pounds.

Agnes, so the prevailing myth goes, was Karen's most powerful prophylactic against the world's lascivious gaze. But we often fail to consider whether or not Karen herself even wanted the attention to her femininity and body, sexual or not, that Agnes is blamed for deflecting without her daughter's consent. Perhaps Karen wanted to preserve some vestige of her tomboyish androgyny—a self-presentation that redirected the lecherous male gaze away from her body, keeping the focus on her talents and abilities. Maybe, just maybe, she still wanted to be thought of as a "player," as a musician, and not as the beautiful girl singer with a beautiful voice. Maybe for Karen being truly seen meant not being reduced to her physique. A Carpenter family friend, Evelyn Wallace, noticed Karen sunbathing in the backyard in Downey one afternoon in 1975, and was taken aback by her spectral, unsexed figure: "You couldn't tell whether it was a girl or a boy. She had absolutely no breasts."[13]

While there are numerous conflicting studies about anorexia and gender presentation, a common through-line across medical and psychological studies is the notion that anorexia is deeply bound up with sufferers' own perceptions of how their femininity is received and interpreted. A brief item in the *British Journal of Medicine* from 1978, contemporaneous with the height of Karen's own struggles with the disease, considers the question, "Anorexia Nervosa: Fear of Fatness or Femininity?"[14] The item does not, as the title suggests, make a definitive choice between the two fears, but instead describes two expressions of the disease that are motivated to either shrink the breasts and hips ("fear of femininity") or reduce one's torso and waist ("fear of fatness").

We will never truly unearth the root causes of Karen's struggles with anorexia. The pains and pathologies are undoubtedly multiple and contorted. But the possibility that she wished, in some way, to unsex her own body, and thus shelter it from scrutiny, remains plausible given everything else we know about her early life and how often she chafed against gender constraints. For all the attention she purportedly craved from the intimates who denied it to her, some part of her also wanted to refuse the attention of a world that demanded the model normalcy she never could—never wanted to—live up to.

* * *

"Are you a boy or a girl?"

This is, perhaps, the most frequently asked question of my life. It began when I was a little kid in Manila who refused to wear the itchy, frilly polyester frocks my mother purchased to doll me up. I preferred the comfort and breathability of cotton pajama pants with tank tops, sometimes with a towel tucked in the back of the tank to serve as a cape for "flying" (inspired by my favorite hero, Superman). My hair also proved confounding. I was given the standard-issue unisex bowl cut for small children in the 1970s, which my mom used to describe to our hairdresser as "the apple look." The bulky shagginess of it irritated me in the prickly heat of the tropics, so I constantly wet it down, making every effort to keep it slicked back with a comb.

Before people began asking me this question directly, they used to ask it of my mother. "Girl or boy?" I could tell it embarrassed her, and she devoted herself to adorning me with the proper feminine accouterments so that she wouldn't be asked anymore. Plastic pink barrettes with flowers and headbands with outsized bows clung to my head like gaudy prostheses meant to verify that I was, indeed, a girl. Mom also acquired many pairs of khaki culottes for me, the chosen compromise for bottoms that offered the mobility of pants or shorts but still looked like a skirt. A skort. At the very least, culottes mimicked the triangle shape on the woman graphic in front of all the public restrooms, the crucible for gender conformity and propriety.

It's not that I ever wanted to be an actual boy, despite my penchant for toy guns and peeing standing up. (It felt dirty to have to sit down, especially in public restrooms.) I merely wanted freedom from the discomforts and constraints of femininity, not being able to move around, take up space, pee anywhere you want, and speak above a whisper.

My mother's femininity was never in any doubt. Elizabeth "Maria" Katindig was a bona fide Filipina debutante. She had her "debut" at the age of sixteen, only a couple of years before she had me. In pictures from that momentous event, which introduced her to Manila as a woman of society, she is every inch the ice queen in a twinkling but understated tiara, a fitted floor-length white dress appliquéd with luminous beads and hand-embroidered flowers, and elbow-length evening gloves. Later in her life, my grandmother complained to me that my mom would go out shopping for dresses imported from Hong Kong, only to sign these purchases to my grandmother's accounts at sundry boutiques around town.

My mother was also always the girl singer: the pretty front woman in elegant gowns with plunging necklines and lots of flare. She performed briefly in a lady trio called Queens of the Night, which specialized in dance music, sequined gowns, and feathered accessories. In more casual rock ensemble settings, she donned brightly patterned Japanese unitards or hip-hugging bell bottoms. In her daily life, she was inspired by Sophia Loren's jet-setting continental attire, with occasional forays into Pucci and the latest trends from Tokyo.

Meanwhile, the Katindig brothers were—still are—bros in every sense of the word: the proverbial mambo kings who played songs of love, with a woman in every resort town in the Pacific Rim, and a few children too. My grandmother would often retell the story of how once, when her car was fogged up in the rain, she reached into the glove compartment to find a cloth to wipe the windshield clean. It turns out the "chamois" she so fortuitously discovered was actually another woman's panties, undoubtedly abandoned in haste by one of my grandfather's other lovers who went for a whirl in his red Benz.

Not a single woman in the Katindig family, except for my mother, ventured into the music business. Her younger brother, Romeo Jr., nicknamed "Boy" (in keeping with the Filipino custom of referring to the first-born male), followed in their father's footsteps and became a jazz pianist. Her uncle Eddie, the aforementioned "Kenny G of the Philippines," also has a jazz pianist son, Eddie Jr., nicknamed "Tateng." My mother was not an instrumentalist, though she would occasionally double on light percussion instruments like cabasas, shakers, and the tambourine.

Because she didn't "play," she was never taken quite as seriously as the boys of her generation in the family. Neither, I expect, would the family have accepted it if she actually declared she wanted to do something like take up the piano, the saxophone (like I did in my teens), or the drums (like Karen). Her singing was appropriate for a pretty, proper, middle-class girl like her, and exactly what she should be doing, nothing more. My mother's musical ambitions never earned the attention or respect of the men in the family, who to this day neglect to consult or invite her when they plan elaborate reunion concerts of the surviving Katindig brothers and their sons. In fact, they'll often hire other, younger female singers for such occasions.

In my mother's case—and I suspect also in the case of many, if not most, other women—achieving a feminine ideal was the source of her profoundest punishments as well as rewards. Or rather, punishment and reward were often interchangeable, and always overlapping. Being a good girl, in every sense of that phrase, means understanding how to excel at a supporting role. Even though she was the lead singer, my mother was also, like Karen, a "lead sister," daughter, and spouse. She absorbed the attention in front, only to facilitate the "genius" all around her that supposedly allowed her to shine—the musicality she "inherited" from her father and uncles, which was somehow never thought of in the same way as the "real" musicianship passed down to her brother and her male cousins. The external validation and attention she might receive from others was meant to be reward enough. Attention from within the family circle was construed as gratuitous, more fodder for her "ego," which shouldn't be allowed to run amok because, after all, she was, and should remain, a good girl.

From the time I was young, it was established that I could never be a good girl like my mother, no matter how tirelessly she tried to correct my comportment and choices in clothing. Queerly, I recoiled from my mother's efforts to untrouble my gender, as well as from the intimacy she tried to forge through "being girls" together. I was vexed by what I perceived to be her vulnerability to the undeserving men in our family, all of whom seemed to take freely but never to give. My grandfather literally took back several gifts he ostentatiously bestowed upon us after he visited us in the States for the first time, in 1985. I really liked that Walkman, and my mom really liked that ring. They were never his to give, I guess. That was the takeaway (pun intended) from his generosity, which was always looked upon admiringly by strangers.

By the time I was an adolescent, the sensation of watching my mother perform became profoundly alienating, almost shame inducing. It cast in relief how troubled my own relationship to gender and performance was—and continues to be. I recall one particularly scarring Fourth of July incident at the Riverside Fireworks Spectacular, held at the football stadium at Riverside Community College. My folks were the headline act. At the age of twelve, with my entire softball team of tough pubescent girls watching, I endured the spectacle of my mom singing Madonna's "Papa Don't Preach," accompanied by horns, while she danced in a sequined top.

This is probably why it was considerably easier for me to relate to my grandmother, who herself never shied away from attention but whose femininity was honed to a stubborn edge of nonconformity. On her wedding day to my grandfather—a day she never wanted but was conscripted into on account of her "condition" (that of being several months pregnant with my mother)—she cut off all her hair into a blunt, short, *Girl, Interrupted*–style 'do. I always admired her for defiling her own showcase femininity on the day her future as a wife and mother was to be consecrated under the watchful eyes of god and the Roman Catholic Church.

The fact that my namesake was a storied tomboy was never lost on me, even when I was a small child. It filled me with the hope that there was some unspoken intelligence or foreknowledge in my mother's act of naming me after a low-voiced woman, with a face more handsome than pretty, who played the drums. Of course, christening me Karen probably had nothing to do with that, and everything to do with how my mother identified with her as a good (young) girl, with a good voice, who had a brother who was also good at playing the piano. But I like to think that it was the first of many accidental, then ultimately intentional, gestures of queer acceptance on her part, despite my own staunch resistance to the femininity she represented and wanted me to represent.

* * *

After her death in 1983, Karen achieved the status of a symbol, of a martyr, not only to various incarnations of control gone awry but also to the prescriptions of femininity and the repression demanded of "good girls" like her. She was, after all, the poster child of "being good" in an era when many radicalized women dared to be bad.[15] Janis Joplin, who died the autumn after "(They Long to Be) Close to You" ruled the summer *Billboard* charts, was in many respects a foil for—indeed, an unruly ancestor to—Karen Carpenter. Janis, too, is characterized as a tragic figure: a martyr to her own follies, a voice of her generation, the hard to Karen's soft.[16]

The Mamas and the Papas' Cass Elliot elicits the most frequent comparisons to Karen, for reasons that are a bit too on the nose. Both died at the age of thirty-two from heart failure, only in Cass's case, "obesity" was considered the cause. Both had distinct alto voices that extended into a stunning range. Drag queens have competed in mock showdowns between Cass and Karen (see San Francisco's "The Monster Show: Cass Elliot versus Karen Carpenter"), and crude jokes circulated about how we could've saved Karen by giving her the ham sandwich Cass was falsely rumored to have choked on when she died. Both women failed at femininity with their competing expressions of excess, overconsumption versus underconsumption, belying the pathological hungers—desires—that made each of them miss a mark very minutely calibrated by the men who ruled the world, the record companies, and their lives.

It is little wonder that (potentially against their will) women like Cass and Karen are posthumously bestowed with such rich, queer afterlives by fans and listeners who hear something in their voices, which desperately want more than heaven or earth allows. Cass's voice, true to form, boomed that struggle to life with or without a mic, filling music halls with the most sonorous of untamed yawps. Karen's voice conveyed its magic through the intimate mediation of microphones, capturing the tiniest of inflections, rasps, fries, and hitches of the throat; a conduit for that tumult of spirit kept so tightly within but breathed to us in the warmest of whispers.

In September 2017, at the venerable Joe's Pub in Manhattan, Mx. Justin Vivian Bond, the New York–based gender-nonconforming cabaret superstar described by *Time Out: New York* as "part transgender den mother, part cultural assassin, part offhand Cassandra," performed a program devoted to Karen, called *Down on Creation—On Top of the World with the Carpenters*. In Mx. Bond's segue between "Someone Like You" and "For All We Know," they confessed that they were attracted to Karen from a young age.

"Did you know," asked Mx. Bond, "that Karen was very butch in presentation and movement?" The very queer crowd, some of whom I knew quite well, tittered with a delighted knowingness. Mx. Bond continued by talking about their tomgirlish adventures with their tomboyish cousin in the country, attributing their future "wet dreams about lesbian friends" to an early love for Karen's drumming.

Karen's queer iconicity for Mx. Bond, for me, for the others in the audience that night, and for many others, including the creators of *Superstar*, Todd Haynes and Cynthia

Schneider (the latter attended Mx. Bond's performance that evening), may appear to be fashioned entirely from fantasy and projection. We queers are really good at that sort of thing, as Oscar Wilde implies in *The Art of Lying*, which he describes as "the telling of beautiful untrue things."

But I want to insist here and now that our fantasies are forged just as much from the facts of our shared intelligence, which are far from being untrue even if they aren't always grounded in what is verifiable fact. What we have learned from Karen, what we share with Karen (beyond the drumming, roughhousing, and sometimes dysphoric relationship to our own bodies) is the experience of living, as anyone who's ever sought acceptance and love has, by trying desperately to get something right. That something will always remain elusive even if we are good. Even if we are perfect. Even if, for just a moment, we can see beyond the horizon.

– 6 –

MADE IN AMERICA

KAREN CARPENTERS OF THE PHILIPPINES

Only diehard Carpenters fans continued to pay much attention to what the duo were up to after 1977, the year they released their last studio album of the decade. A long gap ensued between 1977's *Passage* and the Carpenters' next studio album, *Made in America*, in 1981. This lengthy (for them) hiatus was a result of their necessary retreat into privacy, into rehab programs, psychotherapy, and other concerted efforts to assuage the afflictions that freighted the final years of their imperial ascendancy as pop stars. In most of the made-for-TV biopics about the Carpenters, like 1989's *The Karen Carpenter Story* (for which Richard received codirecting and producing credits), the period between 1977 and 1983 is accelerated and montaged, cataloguing the instances of false hope that Karen would recover—that they would come back bigger than ever—and culminating tragically in her death.

Even though their albums fell precipitously off the charts from diminished radio play, the duo was able to take a more experimental approach with their last album of the 1970s. *Passage* (1977) ambitiously explored an eclectic assortment of genres, from Michael Franks's funky yacht rock tropicália, "Bwana She No Home," to their infamous cover of Klaatu's prog rock epic, "Calling Occupants of Interplanetary Craft." Karen even undertook an earnestly theatrical rendition of "Don't Cry for Me Argentina," the marquee ballad from Andrew Lloyd Webber and Tim Rice's Broadway smash *Evita*. The most Carpenters-esque of tracks on that record, a midtempo number with a nostalgic '60s-era chorus called "All You Get from Love Is a Love Song," was meant to be its breakout single, but it failed to get any airplay or traction on the charts.

The Carpenters saw *Passage* as an expression of liberation, as a declaration of their artistic merits and a stylistic range that would attest to the true depth beneath the hard shellac of their sugarcoated pop exterior. Such strivings to be "taken seriously" were mocked by some critics who were turned off by the thirstiness of their efforts. In a review soaked with sarcasm, the *Milwaukee Journal*'s Joel McNally cynically portrays *Passage* as Richard's ruthlessly calculated yet also desperate bid for artistic recognition: "You get this image of Richard (who chooses and arranges this variety of material) searching frantically for the most unlikely stuff to do, and then Karen singing it just like Karen Carpenter. On 'Two Sides,' Karen laments 'that there is another side of me.' It is her left side and it looks quite a bit like the right side."[1]

The Carpenters were more candid about the premeditated nature of their experimental forays than critics like McNally give them credit for. In a 1978 interview for *Claude Hall's International Radio Report*, a music and radio industry trade publication founded by the legendary *Billboard* columnist who coined the phrase *easy listening*, Karen and Richard fess up to the contortions they'd undergone to find their way back into the Top 40. Exasperated, Karen admits, "We just don't know what Top 40 radio is looking for. One minute they say they're looking for a traditional Carpenters record. We give them one of those and they don't want it. They say they want something different, so we give them 'Occupants' and they don't want that either. . . . If somebody would just let us know what the problem is, then we could take it from there."[2]

For his part, Richard was adamant about the "fickleness" of the American public and radio's willingness to cater to their whims. He equates the public's "burnout" with the Carpenters to what "happened to Elton John . . . John Denver and the Captain and Tennille," while predicting the red-hot Bee Gees would be the next to take a tumble.[3] His and Karen's attitude of admitting things were beyond their control, only to insist stubbornly that they had the capacity to "take it from there," also speaks to the private pathologies that would ultimately undo each of them as the 1970s came to a close.

Shrinking sales weren't the only reason the Carpenters took a much-needed hiatus from studio albums in the final years of the decade. Richard's quaalude addiction had reached a critical status. By January 1979, after abruptly cancelling in the middle of their extended MGM Grand engagement in Las Vegas, Karen helped Richard check into the Menninger chemical dependency unit in Topeka, Kansas. Karen, too, continued to degrade. Despite her intimates' hopes that she would also seek professional treatment, she continued to deny she had anorexia, attributing her health woes to the colitis with which she was diagnosed at the time of her first collapse in 1975.

In 1979, with Richard in rehab, Karen undertook her first major solo project, with serious resistance from her brother, who behaved as though it was an act of betrayal. He eventually relented, grudgingly giving Karen his blessing but making her promise that she wouldn't "do disco." Karen did disco. Or, truer to form, disco lite. She was thrilled with the final product, produced by Phil Ramone, who worked with Paul Simon, Billy Joel, and Barbra Streisand, among other solo pop luminaries of the age.

Karen recorded the album in New York, at A&R records, in the bustle of midtown Manhattan, away from the familiarity of Hollywood's A&M, where she and her brother had spent most of their young adulthood. The record was already scheduled by A&M for release in 1980, and Karen was eager to share the finished product with her family, especially with Richard, and with Herb Alpert and Jerry Moss. She would greet the new decade as an independent woman, free, with her own voice, and with a newly acquired urbanity, sophistication, and maturity.

Richard hated the record. Herb Alpert and Jerry Moss agreed with Richard. To this day, in interviews on television and in print, Richard insists Karen's vocal keys were too high and that she borrowed too liberally from the Carpenters' harmonic sound, as if he had exclusive rights to the overdubbing of her voice. Olivia Newton-John, one of Karen's closest confidantes, was taken aback by Richard's brash claims to ownership during a listening session for the album: "He said to Karen, 'You've stolen the Carpenters' sound.' And I always remember that because—well, she IS the Carpenters sound! Even though he might have thought up the harmonies and everything else, it was her voice that made that sound."[4]

Karen's big brother also objected to the sexual explicitness of the lyrics that transmuted the wholesome closeness for which the Carpenters were known to a full-blown "Making Love in the Afternoon" with Peter Cetera, accompanied by strummy rock guitars and growling, predatory saxophones. Richard complained that "Phil's idea of maturity was to have her singing explicit lyrics. . . . Paul Williams wrote fine lyrics for 'Rainy Days and Mondays' and 'We've Only Just Begun' without any gratuitous reference to sex. Ramone had her singing 'My Body Keeps Changing My Mind.' Is that supposed to be mature?"[5]

Because of Richard's and the record label's less-than-enthusiastic response to Karen's solo effort, the album was shelved, not to be exhumed until 1996, after relentless pressure from Karen's fans who wished to honor her legacy. The eponymous record affects a tone of urbanity distinct from the California sound of lush harmonies Richard established for the Carpenters in Downey and Long Beach under the influence of his choral guru, Frank Pooler, and the bands he loved, like the Beach Boys. In many respects, *disco* was Richard's code word for an "urban" sensibility—dance music (which the Carpenters never performed as a group) from a gay, black, and white-ethnic underground, mainstreamed for the Me Decade's swinging suburbanites. At one point, Richard even referred to the *Karen Carpenter* album as "too New York," doubling down on his disdain for its seediness, spawned as it was from the loins of that grittiest of cities, especially in the '70s when Times Square was more about porn and prostitutes than about the world's largest Olive Garden.

"Lovelines," the album's opening track, both touches upon Richard's fears and makes a mockery of them. The beat is recognizably disco, but its production value, replete with mannered strings and horns hovering above its neutered slap bass, wah-wah guitar, and four-on-the-floor hi-hat, would be more at home on, say, *The Love Boat* than at Studio 54 or San Francisco's Trocadero Transfer. The rest of the album is eclectic, to be sure, though one would be hard pressed to describe it as "too disco," given that Karen's vocal approachability and mellowness on most of the tracks comes closer to quiet storm—a post-1975 genre of slow jams and relaxed rhythms that music critic Rashod Ollison describes as "a showcase for the more sophisticated side of black pop, reflective of the then-expanding black middle class."[6] Karen's voice was fundamentally too bourgie to really get down with disco.

I think it's fair to say that "too New York" or "too disco" translates as "too black" for Richard's comfort—the exact opposite of the Carpenters' (white) bread and butter of love songs and songs you sway to without really moving your ass. While Karen may have dabbled with some of the generic conventions of disco and quiet storm, the record overall doesn't achieve a blue-eyed soulfulness. This is owed in large part to Karen's approach to vocal phrasing, as well trained as she was to remain solidly on the beat, in keeping with the click track, even when a number calls for falling behind or screeching a little bit ahead. The most successful tracks on *Karen Carpenter* are on the (soft) rock end of the spectrum, including her duet with Cetera and the guitar-heavy "Still in Love with You," which would fit seamlessly into Rick Springfield's early '80s repertoire.

As with the Carpenters' Cal State Long Beach choir mentor, Frank Pooler, who for many years avoided gospel and spirituals because of his "lack of familiarity," black genres like disco and soul possibly filled Richard with a racialized anxiety about relinquishing the mastery and perfection at the core of the Carpenters' musical identity. Karen's experiments with musical autonomy in New York, then, were cast as fundamentally unsafe in these terms, along the axes of genre, race, and sensibility—much as the "urban" is always characterized as dangerous territory compared to the carefully regulated, redlined safety of the suburbs.

Shelving her album, at a great financial loss to her individually (upward of $400,000), not only kept Karen a Carpenter, in the musical sense, but it also reinscribed her domestication and suburbanity in both her private and public worlds. It kept the hallmarks of her whiteness unsullied, which, if you listen to the record, was never really in peril. It never really could be. I find it all too fitting that what would become the Carpenters' last studio album—the last record of Karen's abbreviated lifetime—would insistently declare what we always heard to be painfully true in all of their records, "Bwana," "Jambalaya," or no: the Carpenters were *Made in America*.

* * *

In 2007, I went back to where I was made. I had my first *balikbayan* or "homecoming" journey to Manila as a grown-up without parental chaperones. *Balikbayan* translates literally as "return to country" but refers in a more spiritual and colloquial sense to homecoming, to the many Filipinos living permanently abroad who implicitly always have a country to return to. In preparation for this momentous trip, I leafed through a current edition of the Lonely Planet guide at a Borders bookstore after having lunch with my dad.

This is what I learned about my people, at least as they are viewed through the eyes of a plucky travel writer:

> Despite years of injustice at the hands of colonial and homegrown rulers, and despite being for the most part dirt poor, Filipinos are the happiest people in Asia. This incongruous *joie de vivre* is perhaps best symbolized by that quirkiest of national icons, the jeepney. Splashed with colour, laden with religious icons and festooned with sanguine scriblings, the jeepney openly flaunts the fact that, at heart, it's a dilapidated, smoke-belching pile of scrap metal. Like the jeepney, poor Filipinos face their often dim prospects in life with a laugh and a wink.[7]

It struck me then that even though this *Lonely Planet* staff writer observed the cultural incongruity between Filipinos' poverty and joy in a somewhat flippant manner, they managed to stumble upon a truth: one that revealed to me how this alleged Filipino orientation to joy amidst despair could be seen as a negative for the picture perfection modeled by the Carpenters, for their profound despair underlying an intense California sunniness.

While wallowing in my sentimental *balikbayan* journey, I was awash in the music scored by the collective DJs of everyday life in the Philippines: the taxi and jeepney drivers blasting their radios; the "Palawan Idol" winner singing Extreme's "More Than Words" and Jobim classics between shifts tending a beach bar; the Manila municipal government's swanky sound systems piping soothing soft rock into Rizal Park, the city's monument to the slain national hero José Rizal.

I heard the Carpenters everywhere.

I heard "Sing" on the radio at Baclaran market, "We've Only Just Begun" performed by a cover band in Malate, "Close to You" strummed on the guitar in the resort town of Boracay, and countless other incidents since lost to memory. In each instance, almost everyone around sang or hummed along, some under their breath, others with full-throated abandon. Perhaps it was all part of the buildup for Richard Carpenter's scheduled visit to the Philippines a few months later, in 2008. My subsequent visits have assured me, though, that this was—and still remains—an everyday occurrence.

If fewer people in the United States paid attention to the Carpenters after 1977, the rest of the world never stopped listening to them on the radio, even when—or especially when—they took proggy turns with interplanetary travelers in between forays into country and remakes of the hits of yore. Asked whether or not the international radio market remained as big for the Carpenters in 1978 as in the early '70s, Karen responded, "Yes, very big . . . 'Calling Occupants of Interplanetary Craft' was the number one most played album in Japan and 'Sweet, Sweet Smile' is coming on like gangbusters in Germany."[8] Beloved as they were and still are all over the world, there is no place on earth where the Carpenters achieved the kind of radio ubiquity that they longed for back in 1978 as much as they did, in perpetuity, in the Philippines.

To this day, the Carpenters hold the special distinction of being among the few American acts who boast Philippine-only radio hits: album tracks largely unknown in other parts of the world but on heavy rotation on Filipino radio, thus elevating these lesser cuts to the prime status of the artists' more recognizable global hits. As Glenn Tuazon explains in the *Manila Review*: "Never released as a single and apparently deemed a throwaway album cut from *A Kind of Hush*, [the Carpenters' 'You'] reaped a different level of popularity in the Philippines, due to its heavy radio airplay. . . . The song is often the lead track in locally produced Carpenters compilations, which is strange, considering the Carpenters and their label never considered 'You' among the band's best or most important songs."[9]

On Valentine's Day 2008, almost twenty-five years to the day since Karen's death, Richard was enlisted to serenade the sitting Philippine president, Gloria Macapagal Arroyo, at Malacañang Palace, the state residence. Though Arroyo and her cronies were mired in scandal and corruption, the national paper, the *Philippine Daily Inquirer*, reported that "Singing with Carpenter 'saves the day' for Arroyo," noting that Arroyo "broke into song with lyrics evocative of the tumult besetting her administration."[10] Arroyo sang a ballad, "I Have You," from *A Kind of Hush* (1976), a post–imperial phase album consisting mostly of covers, with only three original songs by Richard and John Bettis.

Indeed, most of the Carpenters' records consisted of covers—or more accurately, Richard's arrangements of others' hits—with only a few original Carpenter-Bettis gems sprinkled throughout. The Carpenters, in this sense, differed from some of their peers who also ruled the pop charts in the early '70s: figures like Elton John, Carole King, James Taylor, and Neil Diamond, who brought singer-songwriters to the center stage of pop music.

Maybe this lack of ownership over "originals" also explains why Filipinos have been much kinder to Richard than most in the wake of Karen's death. Richard's sense of "authorship" isn't as much a priority in our nation: a place where achieving precision through an intimate interpretation is a point of pride after a long colonial history in which "mimicry" has been heralded as our greatest skill.[11] Richard is accepted in the Philippines for being a consummate arranger: for knowing how best something should be scored, sung, performed—something he yearned to receive credit for from the Carpenters' broader audiences but only earned from specialists and industry insiders, while Karen was awash in the public's adoration. Just maybe, during Richard's visit to the Philippines in 2008, he brought with him an implicit fantasy that Karen's voice could be brought to life again in another vessel, another body. Such ghostly possessions and vocal reanimations, after all, were not uncommon in our collective experiences of music—of getting right, and making better, voices that had long since disappeared.

Also performing with Richard Carpenter during his visit to the capital was Claire de la Fuente, one among several artists since the 1970s who share the distinction of being dubbed by the press (and their own publicists) as "the Karen Carpenter of the Philippines." De la Fuente earned this title, as her Facebook page explains, because "her voice has a striking resemblance to that of the late singer." While he was in Manila, Richard invited de la Fuente to record a song he originally composed for Karen to sing before she passed away, "Something in Your Eyes," which was first featured on his 1987 solo album, *Time*, with Dusty Springfield filling in the vocal track Karen didn't live to record.

De la Fuente's version, which is actually a cover of what is already an ersatz rendition of a song whose original voice disappeared, amalgamates Karen's and Dusty's vocal styles. With a slight Tagalog accent, de la Fuente evokes Dusty's late-1980s-era wear and tear with her unintentional rasp, while her phrasing shadows the way Karen scooped her notes down from the melodic sweet spots to sit hard on the lower tones of her register with that signature wide vibrato. She also employs some of the vocal enunciations—those vowels with a "Disneyland smile" Frank Pooler writes about in his article on the Carpenters' choral style. Despite a lot of hullabaloo in the Filipino press about Richard Carpenter and Claire de la Fuente's collaboration, her version of "Something in Your Eyes," and her album that bore the same title, failed to turn de la Fuente into an "international singing sensation," as several news outlets hyperbolically predicted.

Five years later, another "Karen Carpenter of the Philippines" was discovered in an arena distinctly removed from the Philippine recording industry—and the presidential palace. The Carpenters' song "You," not to be confused with "I Have You," the song President Arroyo performed with Richard in 2008, is the Philippine-only radio hit that turned Anna Gusmo, an impoverished and blind Manila busker, into a viral video sensation during the summer of 2013. Like scores of other Filipinos who gained transnational notoriety on YouTube—from the Cebu Provincial Rehabilitation and Detention Center inmates, who reenacted the Michael Jackson oeuvre, to Arnel Pineda, the lead singer for Journey whom Neil Schon found online after several failed efforts at finding another post-Perry singer for the band—Gusmo too was "discovered" on that platform, though her story makes apparent some of the true limits of this road to fame.

Gusmo, her husband, Nante, who is also blind, and several other relatives perform daily at the Pasig Public Market in Manila to earn tips to live on as well as to collect donations for the blind. On February 27, 2013, a shopper by the name of Angel Siawingco captured video of Gusmo singing "You" on his cell phone and posted it on YouTube with the label "Karen Carpenter You Sung by Blind Woman."[12] Siawingco's grainy cell phone video shows Gusmo singing the third track from *A Kind of Hush* (1976) with an uncannily Karen-esque timbre and tone, while sitting in a plastic chair, rocking a toddler back and forth with one hand and holding her mic in the other. Unproduced and unaltered by studio mixing—in fact, the audio quality of the original video is notably awful—Gusmo's voice nevertheless sounds hauntingly familiar, as if Karen had come to reinhabit the unlikeliest (or maybe the likeliest?) of other bodies.

Though Siawingco's video of Gusmo topped out at a little over 40,000 views, all the major Filipino news agencies, such as ABS-CBN and GMA, picked up Gusmo's remarkable story and propagated her fame, not only nationwide but throughout the Filipino diaspora, on international cable networks like TFC (The Filipino Channel). Gusmo and her family continued to earn their living through busking, even as her fame and the number of YouTube views of her marketplace performances grew exponentially. When, amidst all the attention, Gusmo was diagnosed with breast cancer, she began seeking donations for her treatment, while several clubs and other entertainment establishments booked her and her all-blind musical ensemble to perform Carpenters covers at fundraisers arranged partly for her benefit.

By 2014 Anna Gusmo usurped Claire de la Fuente as the "Karen Carpenter of the Philippines," as a simple Google search attests, though her financial circumstances remain largely unchanged. Most of the buzz about Karen's voice, and about who truly keeps it alive not only in the Philippines but throughout the Filipino diaspora, is focused on

Gusmo, her rendition of "You," and the melodramatic narration of her blindness. Ironically, "You" is a song about one's total absorption into another's gaze, as well as someone's voice:

Sometimes if I look past you
There's no one beyond your eyes

Ultimately, Karen found no world, no exogamous existence beyond the Carpenters, despite her efforts to do so. And yet in the afterlife of her voice reverberating through numerous Karen Carpenters of the Philippines in various times and places—including those yet to come—we finally find Karen unmoored from the cloistered worlds of whiteness and promises that kept her solo ambitions quashed.

The uncanniness of Gusmo channeling Karen's voice has convinced me that, despite all material evidence to the contrary, the Carpenters may have been—just like me—made in the Philippines, not in America as their last studio album proclaims. Karen stumbled upon the "low voice" by happenstance, through Richard's rearrangement of other people's music, once sung by other women's voices, like "Close to You," the Burt Bacharach tune originally performed by Dionne Warwick in 1963. Such a scrambling of origins would also make sense of McNally's strange assertion that Karen was, in essence, imitating herself—"Karen [was] singing it just like Karen Carpenter"—in his review of *Passage* for the *Milwaukee Journal*.

The Carpenters, in other words, like the Filipinos who loved them then and now, became originals by making the most beautiful copies, sometimes of themselves. Richard's complaints about Karen "stealing the Carpenters' sound" in her solo album underscores their capacity for self-replication and internecine thieving. Though Karen's voice, and the Carpenters' flawless studio sound, are deemed inimitable by most critics—I'm even guilty of making that assertion several times throughout this book—the Karen Carpenters of the Philippines make it abundantly clear just how little that criterion matters, especially in the hands of those among us who are used to transforming what we have, and sometimes the little we've been given, into something far more remarkable.

— 7 —

NOW

Though *Made in America* was the final Carpenters album recorded to completion, their last official studio album is the posthumously released *Voice of the Heart* from October 1983, seven months after Karen's death shook the world. The album features two songs from her final recording sessions and a sampling of unreleased tracks from previous sessions through the years. Of those two songs, the opening track, "Now," was reportedly accomplished in a single take in 1982.

In retrospect, "Now" is to Karen as "I Felt a Funeral in My Brain" (poem 340) is to Emily Dickinson. One cannot help but sense an eerie prescience to a song that opens with the line "Now when it rains I don't feel cold." The rest of what is, true to form, her last love song explains to us that the reason she can't feel the cold, the wind, or the rain is because she's finally found someone else to make her fears and discomfort seem inconsequential. As with most of her other love songs about achieving such flawless, bonded intimacies, it was only just a dream, a speculative fiction about a future that had to exist somewhere else, on another plane, in another dimension. The inscription on the mausoleum she shares with her parents reads A STAR ON EARTH—A STAR IN HEAVEN, fashioning some equivalency between the life she led here and whatever the afterlife promises, though I can't help but think she would want something radically different from the life she led bounded by this world.

It's not so unusual to feel haunted by the voices of singers we've lost too soon, and unexpectedly, even if such losses aren't quite as unexpected in the harsh glare of further reflection. Nevertheless, the magnitude to which we—to which I—feel haunted by Karen has a special character because of the enduring hope and yearning that suffuses so much of what her voice brought to life, and because so many others have tried to reanimate that voice in tribute albums, through idiosyncratic covers, and sometimes, as Anna Gusmo showed us, through uncanny imitations in the old colonial outposts of America. Karen haunts us with (to use the words of the preeminent queer theorist Lauren Berlant) her "cruel optimism."[1] Simply put, Berlant describes cruel optimism as a persistent attachment to the very things that are at once the source of our optimism as well as the barrier to its fulfillment and our thriving.

We can trace Karen's cruel optimism not only in her biography, through the family from whom she sought the unconditional love she never quite received, but also in her music—in the songs she sang that taught us to abide by our own cruel optimism about true love, auspicious beginnings, and a perfect "now" we might never live to see. The cruelty of Karen's optimism was, and continues to be, what makes it so infectious. It is why our attachment to her, my attachment to her, is tinged with such a prevailing sense of sadness as well as joy. If Karen was the voice of her generation—and I believe she was—her brief life and her enduring music leave that generation, as well as the many who followed, with a jarring realism about just how far our dreams might take us, which is never far enough.

To this day, Karen's "heart"—a giant rose-colored crystal purchased by Herb Alpert in the late 1990s—remains illuminated at all hours in the former A&M Studio B, now the Henson Recording Studios, in Hollywood, California. Dubbed "the Karen Carpenter room," Studio B is a tracking room geared to live sound recordings. It was among her favorites and was the site of many of the Carpenters' recordings, as well as all the sessions for Carole King's *Tapestry*. Tales abound of Karen's ghostly visitations to Studio B, even after A&M was acquired by Polygram Records in 1989, and even after the Henson Company purchased the property a decade later, in 1999, when A&M's official operations ceased (until their revival as a trademarked brand in 2007).

When I visited Studio B in September 2017, Faryal Ganjehei, studio manager and vice president of Henson Studio operations, shared a few stories about some of the strange occurrences throughout the years that led to the perpetual illumination of the crystal Alpert dubbed "Karen's heart."

The mixing dials would mysteriously move. Lights would flicker. Buttons untouched by human hands would suddenly depress. Visiting the studio stirred some of the same feelings I had when I walked by the duhat tree my grandmother paid the curandera to exorcise in our Manila carport. Sure, it could've just been the power of suggestion; but the shadows cutting across the massive rose quartz anchored to the center of the wall suggested a presence that filled me with a slight dread, as well as titillation.

The gossip outlet TMZ.com even made a joke segment out of one of the Studio B incidents by speculating that the ghost of murdered rap legend Tupac Shakur also showed up at the studio to "ghost bone" Karen Carpenter. The hip-hop artist and producer DJ Quick told TMZ that a sinister laughter appeared on one of the tracks he recorded in the studio as he was sampling Tupac's work.[2] Tellingly, TMZ's bro patrol didn't even think of attributing the haunting to Karen herself. They collectively conjured Tupac as a spectral hook-up for her instead, endowing Karen with a slightly raunchier, more racially exogamous afterlife than her family, and many of her fans, would dare to imagine.

Rescripting Karen's afterlife is a game in which quite a few of us have indulged. I'm guilty of doing some of it here in this book. It's one thing to acknowledge the legacy of her remarkable voice and the lasting influence her distinctive alto had on singers across genres and generations. It's another to endow Karen with some sort of cool cred: an edgier afterlife, less sheltered, racially homogenous, and straight (in many senses of that term) than the one she actually lived. This is why some of the more recent covers of the Carpenters' most beloved songs—some of which were also covers themselves—also try, perhaps a bit too hard, to establish dramatically different settings that are a far cry from Richard's masterfully planned arrangements.

In 1994, twenty years after the Carpenters' commercial peak, twenty-five years after their first A&M record, and over a decade after Karen's death, the indie and alternative rock impresarios Matt Wallace and David Konjoyan compiled a tribute album of the Carpenters' greatest hits. Riffing on the title of a well-known Tim Hardin song, *If I Were a Carpenter* is a covers compilation to which many music critics of the 1990s attribute the Carpenters' rehabilitation among the jaded cool kids of Generation X. Wallace and Konjoyan noticed some favorable comments about the Carpenters swirling around the music press from indie darlings like Sonic Youth and Babes in Toyland. A&M was eager to commemorate the Carpenters' twenty-fifth anniversary and enlisted Wallace and Konjoyan, who described themselves as "simply fans" of the Carpenters, to bring together an impressive roster of some of the hottest alternative acts of the moment, including Sonic Youth, Bettie Serveert, Shonen Knife, and American Music Club.

Since the album was crafted during the early '90s age of irony, Richard was concerned it might actually turn out to be a send-up: "After the initial meeting, I didn't think about it at all. . . . Then a couple of articles came out saying this was being done so they could make fun [of us]."[3] After advanced access to some rough cuts, Richard decided, "They struck me as honest."[4] In his interview with Richard for *HITS* magazine, it's with a sense of pride that Konjoyan asks the surviving elder Carpenter whether or not he feels the tribute album is a "vindication," because "artists who are sort of the pillars of cool today" elected to participate. In his characteristically cocksure fashion, Richard had little doubt about his and the Carpenters' legacy: "I think what this might do is at least show to some people that our music has a little more appeal to varying tastes than might have been thought." It's a line that echoes some of the retorts he offered in interviews throughout the '70s, particularly during some of their post-imperial struggles at the end of that decade.

On the whole, over twenty years later, *If I Were a Carpenter* sounds a bit more like a novelty album than it did when I first eagerly and earnestly consumed it in 1994. The Cranberries' "Close to You" and Shonen Knife's "Top of the World" are pretty straightforward riffs on the originals, albeit in the idiom of melodic '90s pop. The "deepest" track, and the one that continues to receive the most attention from the compilation, is Sonic Youth's rendition of "Superstar," which I find unnecessarily dour, and ironically somewhat overwrought in its understatedness. Even though "Superstar" is among the Carpenters' most beloved songs, and arguably one of their most haunting numbers, Karen herself didn't much care for it. As Richard explains,

"I had to persuade her for about a week. . . . I said, 'Karen, FOR ME, PLEASE do this one!'"[5] She eventually grew to love the finished product.

Many of the artists featured on *If I Were a Carpenter* took liberties with either an excessive cheeriness they associated with the duo or a kind of somberness, as Sonic Youth modeled, in a nod to the tragedy of Karen's death. The most effective effort at such moodiness on *If I Were a Carpenter* belongs to Bettie Serveert's "For All We Know." The Dutch rockers managed to make the song conform to their signature sound of swooping, off-kilter guitars and fuzz, without contorting the sentiments of the original. Carol Van Dijk, their lead singer, figured out how to make her laconic vocal style resonate with Karen's phrasing, which some listeners tend to hear as "emotive," but which usually comes across to others as even-keeled or emotionally unperturbed.

I was a senior in college when *If I Were a Carpenter* came out, and not especially eager to brandish my love of the Carpenters' original music to my Sonic Youth–worshipping classmates, who already mocked my fandom of "pop" bands like 10,000 Maniacs. I did, however, exact sweet revenge on some wannabe frat-bro neighbors who lived upstairs when, the morning after they threw an all-night rager, I blasted the Carpenters' "Sing" at full volume from my giant '80s-era Kmart speakers. A decade into living in America and I was still afraid my predilection for soft rock—cleverly concealed beneath the guise of the resurrected women's alt-folk of the era by the Indigo Girls, Ani DiFranco, Sarah McLachlan, and people like Natalie Merchant of 10,000 Maniacs—would reveal my provincial origins in the suburbs, and in another country.

Richard could not have cared less if the Carpenters were refashioned into something "cool" for a new hipsterati, but for *this* Karen, *If I Were a Carpenter* presented an opportunity to reconcile my enduring passions for distinctly uncool music that was not of the moment with something that actually was, or at least promised to be. I'd just come out as a lesbian the year before, and while queerness in general was having its rainbow-flag, rainbow-ringed moment of conditional acceptance in the Clintonian early '90s, lesbianism continued (and continues) to carry with it the stylistic and social burden of being stuck in the past—a kind of "temporal drag," as the queer scholar Elizabeth Freeman describes it.[6] Lesbians, in other words, are never of the moment, or only fleetingly so whenever popular magazines decide it's time for another wave of "lesbian chic." We famously have terrible taste in music, clothes, and fashion, at least compared to cosmopolitan gay men and creative-class elites. Try as I might to buck that image by affecting a Riot Grrrl pose in the early '90s—which consisted of rust-colored shorts and an oversized Dodgers V-neck—I never quite managed it, especially because I would always return to Emily Saliers's sappy ballads from Indigo Girls records, while my more avant peers preferred

Amy Ray's hard-strumming, punk-influenced forays into her stream of consciousness.

Karen Carpenter was my gateway to the delicate song-craft of Emily Saliers, to Sarah McLachlan, and to the other chanteuses of the Lilith Fair circuit in the early to mid-1990s. It is no accident that in the many documentaries produced about the Carpenters from the '90s onward, some of my heroines from that era, like k. d. lang and even Linda Perry of Four Non Blondes, appear in tribute as interview subjects. Straight as she seemed, again, in all senses of the word, Karen was the original coordinate for my queerness. The most normal songs she sang about unrequited longing became my torch ballads for a love that dare not speak its name—for loves I imagined would never come to fruition. That straightness was also bound up with my sense of what might constitute racial and national belonging: my brownness, my gender nonconformity, alienated me from everything in the wheelhouse of normalcy. Karen was my conduit to some idea of how it all might play out, or at least how it's supposed to. Her songs were my conduct manuals for proper behaviors and acceptable passions.

Karen was my funhouse mirror of whiteness and promises, of an American perfection that seemed unattainable, with its sparkling suburban domiciles, political innocence, and hetero scripts of prosperous futures; of a thinness I would never once be able to achieve, and that Karen too could never construe as enough. Karen's own aberrance never made itself apparent to me when I was a kid growing up, going back and forth across the Pacific to seemingly incongruous places that I came to understand were both home. I don't know that I ever truly *heard* the Carpenters, or heard Karen, until I multiplied those crossings, and until I heard her *voice* multiply across and through other bodies that weren't anything like hers. Maybe this is what haunts me, and haunts all of us: that a voice so "inimitable," so one of a kind, can always find another life, another way to resound.

* * *

It's kinda corny to listen back.

—KAREN CARPENTER
in an interview with Ray Coleman for *Melody Maker*, 1975

If I didn't feel "safe" listening to the Carpenters as a cosmopolitan aspirant in college, nothing felt safer to me than revisiting the Philippines in the many years after and coming to the realization that there is likely nowhere else in the world that the Carpenters remain so loved. While the Carpenters mania that seems to exist in perpetuity in the Philippines might be easily (and to a certain extent, rightfully) construed as yet another of the many vestiges of the nation's colonial entanglements with the United States—what the Filipino historian Vicente Rafael describes as *White Love and Other Events in Filipino History* (2000)—I would argue that there is a power relationship more difficult to parse, a different dynamic, another species of intimacy between Karen and my people, Karen and me.

You see, Karen and the Carpenters belong to *us*, not the other way around. Karen's voice is not simply a fetish object of self-annihilating perfection, as the scholar Eric Lott has provocatively argued, nor is it the wet maternal kiss oozing with eros and comfort, as musicologist Mitchell Morris describes.[7] Neither is Karen just another martyr in the sacred and secular cosmologies of Filipino Catholicism.

Journalists have tried to crack the case of why certain "ethnic" communities "worship" seemingly incongruous white singers: for example, the throngs of Latinos in the United States who are bonkers for Morrissey. These same journalists have played the Catholic card before, implying a one-to-one correspondence between religious forms of idolatry, sentimentality, and fandom. But with Karen Carpenter, we aren't just fans, followers, or cheerful colonial acolytes, Kipling's infamous "little brown brothers" worshipping another white woman's prudish perfection. Karen's voice is *our* voice, and as Claire de la Fuente, Anna Gusmo, and countless others before and after them will confirm, we have the power to reanimate her, for better or worse, as *our* echo.

When I am back in Manila and my ears are filled with what I've come to understand as my immigrant love songs, written and performed by American pop stars like the Carpenters, this obfuscation of origins troubles my relationship to space and source. And it is in that headspace of defamiliarization, where one arrives at a clearer sense of the stoniness of the stone (to borrow the grumpy Russian formalist Viktor Shklovsky's words)—or in this instance, the placeness of a place—that I begin to understand what Karen has actually done for me. She is more than my namesake; she is my constant, to crib a concept from the time-bending, and now also outdated, universe of *Lost*. She is the anchor to a *now*, a *then*, a *never was*, and a *never will be*. She is the one who taught me that optimism is cruel, and yet she is the one I remain attached to, despite the inevitable harm such attachments sometimes carry with them.[8] She has always been my gateway to belonging, yet also the harbinger of its foreclosure.

Karen Carpenter's dispassionately passionate vocals multiply not only across the harmonies in her own recordings but also through countless Filipino voices, making sense of both Manila and the Southern California suburbs that became my eventual home. Through Karen, I came to understand that soft rock might not signal a weakness or vulnerability, but instead announce a strength: the audacity to sound out of place and out of time, like someone who isn't made for this world. Someone who's especially corny, not just someone who's old-fashioned or stubbornly clinging to the notion that "every sha-la-la-la, every whoah-wo-oh, still shines." I've always found it apt that Karen Carpenter, the contradiction, helped launch the most soothing of musical oxymorons, soft rock. With a little help from Tony Peluso's melodic fuzz guitar solo in "Goodbye to Love," soft rock became the musical genre that turned on our heartlights across the Pacific and back. Karen created the spark that would inevitably ignite the world with innumerable butane flames.

This is the eternal flame I've carried in my corny heart these many years. For all the reasons Karen Carpenter matters to the world, to us, to me, the most important thing she offered was her unabashed heart—or at least the *idea* that we could ever have access to such a thing from her, from someone, from anyone. Karen's heart looms over whatever else may come from Studio B on the old A&M lot. Its light—because of both the admiration and the fear it inspires—will never be extinguished.

After listening to Karen Carpenter again, and to the many women who have held the title "the Karen Carpenter of the Philippines," I've also begun to hear my mother's voice anew. It ceased to sound like Karen Carpenter's after she abandoned her pop ambitions in order to become a "real musician." She chose to labor under the tyranny of jazz, a pursuit for the musically righteous, not for wage vocalists, which she had been forced to become when we first landed in Southern California. Jazz was a dominion ruled by men like my grandfather and his brothers, who played like angels but disappeared like devils. Though she capitulated to the family business, to the ruin and glory it always promised, she still managed to defy their legacy by naming me after the girl pop singer who also happened to be a girl drummer. A girl who would never be normal, no matter how hard she tried, and no matter how badly she was supposed to want it. A girl who will always be remembered, despite a lifetime of feeling forgotten. A girl who left this world too soon, but who was destined to live forever.

ACKNOWLEDGMENTS

An earlier essay that grew into this book first appeared in *Buzzfeed Reader* in May 2017 and was originally commissioned for a music issue of the *Believer* by two of the magazine's former editors, Karolina Waclawiak and Andi Winnette. I thank them for their early editorial input and generosity. Of course, this book wouldn't even exist without the stewardship and editorial guidance of my series editors, Evelyn McDonnell and Stephen P. Hull, and the University of Texas Press, especially Casey Kittrell, for taking on the Music Matters series when its previous press folded unexpectedly. I thank them for their patience and their willingness to indulge the more experimental aspects of this work.

Contrary to the popular myth that the writing and imagining for a project of this sort happens in isolation, my own process owes so much to the collaborations, both intentional and incidental, that come to fruition through encounters with colleagues and fellow travelers at the annual MoPOP (formerly EMP) Pop Conference, and at my scholarly home, the University of Southern California. Many of them are cited in this book, but additional thanks are owed to people like John Andrews, Lauren Berlant, Sarah Banet-Weiser, Nao Bustamante, Lynne Chan, Virginia Chang,

Jennifer Doyle, Emily Gale, Raquel Guttierez, Lucas Hilderbrand, Leon Hilton, Homay King, Jason King, Yael Kropsky, Josh Kun, Greta LaFleur, Chris Molanphy, Tavia Nyong'o, Katrin Pahl, Hiram Perez, Ann Powers, Iván Ramos, Camille Robcis, Gustavus Stadler, Jennifer Stoever, Neda Ulaby, Jeanne Vaccaro, Alexandra Vazquez, Oliver Wang, Eric Weisbard, Patricia White, Genevieve Yue, Andy Zax, and countless others. Each of you, at one point or another, has let me talk your ears off about this project over drinks and decadent meals, on car rides, and at Mx. Justin Vivian Bond's show about the Carpenters, *Down on Creation* (at Joe's Pub in New York). I'm also grateful to Mx. Bond for taking the time to chat with me at the Library Bar and for sharing my original article on Karen Carpenter with the Carpenters' fans.

Taylor Black, El Glasberg, and Chase Smith kindly accompanied me to the Pierce Brothers Cemetery in Westlake Village, California, on a scorching July afternoon in 2017 so I could pay my respects at Karen Carpenter's mausoleum. The Carpenter family crypt was actually moved from Cypress, California, to Westlake Village in 2003, to be closer to where Richard currently resides. I appreciate Taylor, Glas, and Chase's willingness to share, then process, this profound, sometimes disturbing experience, over pie and sandwiches at Corky's Restaurant in Sherman Oaks.

Faryal Ganjehei and Jaime Sickora at Henson Recording Studios (the former site of A&M Records) generously led me on a tour of Studio B, a space allegedly haunted by Karen's ghost. I'm forever grateful to both of you for showing me Karen's "heart," in crystal form, which I discuss in chapter 7, and for sharing stories about strange occurrences in the studio. A special thanks is owed to Devon Kirkpatrick for alerting me to these ghost stories and for connecting me to Faryal and Jaime.

To the friends and loved ones based in Los Angeles—at least most of the time—who tolerated my repeat-listening of the entire Carpenters oeuvre, as well as my incessant, anxious handwringing about this project: I owe you all a round at Taix, especially Megan Auster-Rosen, Ava Berkofsky, Samantha Cohen, Andrea Fontenot, Shari Frilot, Sarah Johnson, Sabrina Kosok, Jane McCarthy, Moira Morel, Alison Picard, and Sarah Gertrude Shapiro.

My podcast mates at *Pop Rocket*—Guy Branum, Wynter Mitchell, and Margaret Wappler—as well as our producer Laura Swisher and regular guest stars like Alonso Duralde have let me workshop aspects of this book with our listening public. Louis Virtel's arrival on the *Pop Rocket* scene just as I was completing this manuscript was an absolute goddess-send. I had no idea anyone under the age of forty could own that many flatteringly tight Carpenters T-shirts.

In many respects this book is all about my family, without whom nothing I've accomplished is possible. I thank my parents, James Dykes and Elizabeth "Maria" Katindig-Dykes, for accepting my honesty and candor in this book, and throughout my life. I'm also indebted to the

Dykes, Katindigs, Tongsons, and Moraleses who appear in this book, and who've been stalwart keepers of these family stories. I'm very fortunate to have such lovely in-laws, the Kesslers, who have expanded the scope of a relatively small immediate family, to our tremendous delight. My grandmother Linda Katindig died before I really had a chance to dive into this project; I know she would've been tickled by my detours back to 7 General Capinpin Street. I miss her every day and thank her for showing me at an early age what it looked like to write.

A few experimental drafts of this book were coauthored by Lily and Corky, two large, cuddly, bourgeois cats found on the streets of downtown L.A. who have a penchant for computer keyboards. I treasure every day I get to spend with these loving beings, even if it means losing portions of a chapter here and there.

So much of this book is about heartbreak and unrequited love, the Carpenters' aesthetic wheelhouse, as well as the underlying sources of tragedy we tend to read into Karen Carpenter's life story. Despite the sadness and cynicism that permeates this project, and life in general, I am incredibly lucky to have found someone to share "horizons that are new to us." To my spouse and my love, Sarah Kessler, thank you, as always, for being willing to stare into the abyss with me, and for holding my hand as we do so.

NOTES

Preface

1. Though the stricter definition of "namesake" dictates that the person who is named *after* someone would be given that designation (i.e., convention would dictate that I would actually be Karen's namesake, not the way I've written it here, and throughout this book), a more capacious use of the word, noted in both the OED and Webster's, suggests that a namesake can be any "person or thing that has the same name as another." As I hope the rest of this book makes apparent, my relationship to Karen is in the spirit of this more promiscuous model of non-hierarchical kinship and name sharing.

1. Whiteness and Promises

1. *'SusMaryosep* is a colloquial Tagalog contraction for the phrase *Jesus, Mary, and Joseph!*
2. Tom Smucker, "Boring and Horrifying Whiteness: The Rise and Fall of Reganism as Prefigured by the Career Arcs of Carpenters, Lawrence Welk and the Beach Boys in 1973–4," in *Pop When the World Falls Apart: Music in the Shadow of Doubt*, ed. Eric Weisbard (Durham, NC: Duke University Press, 2012), 47–61.
3. *Close to You: The Story of the Carpenters*, BBC documentary (2002).
4. Richie C. Quirino, *Pinoy Jazz Traditions* (Pasig City, Philippines: Anvil, 2004), 140.
5. Randy L. Schmidt, *Little Girl Blue: The Life of Karen Carpenter* (Chicago: Chicago Review Press, 2010), 19.
6. Interview with Ray Moore, BBC Radio, 1981.
7. This assignment scrawled in Karen's own hand was reprinted in Ray

Coleman's *The Carpenters: The Untold Story* (New York: HarperCollins, 1994), 45–47.

8. *The Carpenters' Story: Only Yesterdays*, BBC documentary (2007).

9. Lucas Hilderbrand, "Grainy Days and Mondays: *Superstar* and Bootleg Aesthetics," *Camera Obscura* 19, no. 3 (2004): 56–91.

10. Tom Nolan, "Up from Downey," a feature in *Rolling Stone* (1974), reprinted in *Yesterday Once More: The Carpenters Reader*, ed. Randy L. Schmidt (Chicago: Chicago Review Press, 2012), 101.

11. Dan Armstrong, "Why They're on Top," *Southeast News* (1971), reprinted in *Yesterday Once More: The Carpenters Reader*, 49.

12. Armstrong, "Why They're on Top," 49.

13. Nolan, "Up from Downey," 99.

14. Lester Bangs, "The Carpenters and the Creeps," review in *Rolling Stone* (1971), reprinted in *Yesterday Once More: The Carpenters Reader*, 19.

15. Segment on *The Tonight Show with Johnny Carson*, excerpted on the 2007 BBC documentary *The Carpenters' Story: Only Yesterday*.

16. Bangs, "The Carpenters and the Creeps," 19.

17. Ken Michaels, "Rainy Days and Mondays Always Get Me Down," *Chicago Tribune Magazine* (1971), reprinted in *Yesterday Once More: The Carpenters Reader*, 39.

18. Ibid.

19. Ibid., 45.

20. Ibid., 40.

21. Coleman, *The Carpenters: The Untold Story*, 50.

2. For All We Know

1. Randy L. Schmidt, *Little Girl Blue: The Life of Karen Carpenter* (Chicago: Chicago Review Press, 2010).

2. "Karen Carpenter: Nothing to Hide Behind," radio interview with Charlie Tuna on KIIS FM, October 8, 1976, reprinted in *Yesterday Once More: The Carpenters Reader*, ed. Randy L. Schmidt (Chicago: Chicago Review Press, 2012).

3. Schmidt, *Little Girl Blue*, 26.

4. Ibid., 85.

5. *Jerry Dunphy Visits the Carpenters* (televised interview), February 21, 1972.
6. Rod Fogarty, "Karen Carpenter: A Drummer Who Sang," *Modern Drummer* (2001), reprinted in *Yesterday Once More: The Carpenters Reader*, 55.
7. Interview for the BBC documentary *The Carpenters' Story: Only Yesterday* (2007).

3. Long Beach State of Mind

1. Liner notes from the Carpenters box set, *From the Top*, 1991.
2. Rod Fogarty, "Karen Carpenter: A Drummer Who Sang," in *Modern Drummer* 2001, reprinted in *Yesterday Once More: The Carpenters Reader*, ed. Randy L. Schmidt (Chicago: Chicago Review Press, 2012), 54.
3. Randy L. Schmidt, *Little Girl Blue: The Life of Karen Carpenter* (Chicago: Chicago Review Press, 2010), 30.
4. Their complete finale performance can be found here: "CARPENTERS Your All-American College Show 1968," posted January 28, 2011, by Suntorypop, www.youtube.com/watch?v=XP_WyynSAxw; while excepts of their preliminary performance (mislabeled as taking place in 1966 on the E! Network's footage) is compiled here in a fan video: "Carpenters—Dancing in the Street (1968, good quality)," posted January 10, 2007, by CrescentNoon, www.youtube.com/watch?v=-PAy6Ab3CcQ.
5. Schmidt, *Little Girl Blue*, 40.
6. *From the Top* box set.
7. Jennifer Stoever, *The Sonic Color Line: Race and the Cultural Politics of Listening* (New York: NYU Press, 2016).
8. Schmidt, *Little Girl Blue*, 42.
9. Ibid.
10. Ibid., 43.
11. Frank Pooler, "The Choral Sound of the Carpenters," *The Choral Journal* (1973), reprinted in *Yesterday Once More: The Carpenters Reader*, 58.
12. Schmidt, *Little Girl Blue*, 48.
13. Ibid.

4. Goodbye to Love

1. Randy Schmidt offers a detailed account of how Richard procured the reference disc of the demo for the Crocker Bank commercial and put together the stunning arrangement that became a wedding standard for generations to come. See *Little Girl Blue: The Life of Karen Carpenter* (Chicago: Chicago Review Press, 2010), 59–61.

2. k. d. lang made these remarks on the A&E cable network's 1999 documentary special *Carpenters: Harmony and Heartbreak*.

3. *Little Girl Blue*, 66.

4. For more on radio formats, genres, and how popular tastes were shaped by programmers and other industry insiders, see Eric Weisbard's *Top 40 Democracy: The Rival Mainstreams of American Music* (Chicago: University of Chicago Press, 2014) and Kim Simpson's *Early '70s Radio: The American Format Revolution* (London: Bloomsbury Academic, 2011). For a discussion of the erotic and racialized dimensions of pop music and its cultural history in the United States, see NPR music critic Ann Powers's recent book, *Good Booty: Love and Sex, Black and White, Body and Soul in American Music* (New York: Dey Street, 2017).

5. On August 1, 2017, I conducted an informal poll and discussion thread about the origins of soft rock with music critics and scholars like Andy Zax, Ann Powers, Eric Weisbard, Glenn Hendler, Roshanak Kheshti, and others on Facebook. Zax's quote is pulled directly from that conversation.

6. Peluso made these remarks on *Carpenters: Harmony and Heartbreak*.

7. Quoted in Tony Peluso's obituary in the *Independent*. Peluso died June 5, 2010, from heart disease. He was sixty years old. Pierre Perrone, "Tony Peluso: Guitarist Whose Solos on the Carpenters' 'Goodbye to Love' Ushered in the Power-Ballad Era," *Independent* (UK), August 2, 2010, www.independent.co.uk/news/obituaries/tony-peluso-guitarist-whose-solos-on-the-carpenters-goodbye-to-love-ushered-in-the-power-ballad-era-2041048.html.

8. Ibid.

9. For an amusing fan discussion of the Carpenters' (some say excessive) use of the oboe, see this A&M Music online forum: "The Oboe," A&M Corner, http://forum.amcorner.com/threads/the-oboe.11218.

10. Perry made these remarks in the BBC documentary *Only Yesterday: The Carpenters' Story* (2007).

5. Queer Horizon

1. Ray Coleman, "Carpenters—Good, Clean, All-American Aggro!," in *Melody Maker* 1975, reprinted in *Yesterday Once More: The Carpenters Reader*, ed. Randy L. Schmidt (Chicago: Chicago Review Press, 2012), 154.
2. For more on the genesis and definition of this concept, see music critic Tom Ewing's "Imperial," *Pitchfork*, May 25, 2010, https://pitchfork.com/features/poptimist/7811-poptimist-29.
3. Ibid.
4. Coleman, "Carpenters—Good, Clean, All-American Aggro!," 156.
5. Ibid., 157.
6. Randy Schmidt, *Little Girl Blue: The Life of Karen Carpenter* (Chicago: Chicago Review Press, 2010), 151.
7. Ibid.
8. *The Carpenters' Story: Only Yesterday*, BBC documentary (2007).
9. Rob Hoerburger, "Karen Carpenter's Second Life," *New York Times Magazine*, October 6, 1996, www.nytimes.com/1996/10/06/magazine/karen-carpenter-s-second-life.html. Recorded in 1979–1980 with producer Phil Ramone, Karen's eponymously titled solo album was shelved after Richard, Herb Alpert, and Jerry Moss disapproved of its "disco" leanings and risqué themes. The album wasn't released until thirteen years after she died, in 1996, with a renewed retromania sparking interest in Karen and the Carpenters.
10. "Karen Carpenter: Nothing to Hide Behind," radio interview with DJ Charlie Tuna on KIIS FM, October 8, 1976, reprinted in *Yesterday Once More: The Carpenters Reader*, 185.
11. Carpenters manager Sherwin Bash, quoted in Schmidt, *Little Girl Blue*, 129.
12. Lead Sister has archived its newsletters on their website, with framing commentary at http://leadsister.com. The citation is pulled from "1975,"

Lead Sister, http://leadsister.com/?page_id=135, accessed September 23, 2017.

13. Schmidt, *Little Girl Blue: The Life of Karen Carpenter*, 131.

14. "Anorexia Nervosa: Fear of Fatness or Femininity?" *British Medical Journal* 1.6104 (1978): 5.

15. See Alice Echols's absorbing history *Daring to Be Bad: Radical Feminism in America, 1967–1975* (Minneapolis: University of Minnesota Press, 1989). See also Echols's work on Janis Joplin, *Scars of Sweet Paradise: The Life and Times of Janis Joplin* (New York: Henry Holt, 2000).

16. Though she doesn't explicitly contrast Janis and Karen in her chapter on the 1970s, Ann Powers's formulation about the "hard and soft realities" of 1970s rock inspired my discussion of the two singers. See Powers's *Good Booty: Love and Sex, Black and White, Body and Soul in American Music* (New York: HarperCollins, 2017).

6. Made in America: Karen Carpenters of the Philippines

1. Joel McNally, "The Unwholesome Carpenters," *Milwaukee Journal* (1977), reprinted in *Yesterday Once More: The Carpenters Reader*, ed. Randy L. Schmidt (Chicago: Chicago Review Press, 2012), 214.

2. Bill Moran, "If Somebody Would Just Let Us Know What the Problem Is . . ." *Claude Hall's International Radio Report* (1978), reprinted in *Yesterday Once More: The Carpenters Reader*, 224.

3. Ibid., 226.

4. Quoted in Ray Coleman, *The Carpenters: The Untold Story* (New York: HarperCollins Publishers, 1994), 274.

5. Neil McCormick, "Karen Carpenter and the Mystery of the Missing Album," *London Daily Telegraph*, February 4, 2016, www.telegraph.co.uk/music/artists/karen-carpenter-and-the-mystery-of-the-missing-album.

6. Rashod Ollison, "Causing a Quiet Storm: Radio Format Showcasing Black Pop Music Turns 40," *Virginian Pilot*, July 12, 2015, https://pilotonline.com/entertainment/music/causing-a-quiet-storm-radio-format-showcasing-black-pop-music/article_225a3796-0933-56a4-ba04-6658b80d49c5.html.

7. *Lonely Planet Guide to the Philippines* (Nashville: Lonely Planet, 2006), 33.

8. Moran, "If Somebody Would Just Let Us Know What the Problem Is," 224.

9. Glenn Tuazon, "Hang the DJ: The Demise of the Philippine-Only Radio Hit," *Manila Review*, March 2015, http://themanilareview.com/issues/view/hang-the-dj-the-demise-of-the-philippine-only-radio-hit.

10. Michael Lim Ubac, "Singing with Carpenter 'Saves the Day' for Arroyo," *Philippine Daily Inquirer*, February 15, 2008, http://newsinfo.inquirer.net/inquirerheadlines/nation/view/20080215-118995/Singing-with-Carpenter-saves-the-day-for-Arroyo.

11. I lack the space in this context to address in a scholarly manner the Philippines' long colonial history and its effects on the nation's musical and performance cultures. For more on how the Filipino origins of karaoke are linked to accounts of musical imitation, see my article "Empty Orchestra: The Karaoke Standard and Pop Celebrity" in *Public Culture* 27, no. 1 (January 2015). See also Stephanie Ng's crucial foundational work from 2005, "Performing the 'Filipino' at the Crossroads: Filipino Bands in Five-Star Hotels throughout Asia," in *Modern Drama from 1850 to the Present* 48, no. 2 (Summer 2005), and these book-length studies on colonialism, Filipino performance, and music: Lucy Burns, *Puro Arte: Filipinos on the Stages of Empire* (New York: NYU Press, 2013) and Christine Bacreza Balance, *Tropical Renditions: Making Musical Scenes in Filipino America* (Durham, NC: Duke University Press, 2016).

12. Siawingco's original cell phone video is still accessible on YouTube: "Karen Carpenter You Sung by Blind Woman," April 23, 2013, www.youtube.com/watch?v=we3I5uPXpXE.

7. Now

1. Lauren Berlant, *Cruel Optimism* (Durham, NC: Duke University Press, 2011).

2. "DJ Quick: I Was Haunted by . . . Tupac and Karen Carpenter!!" on TMZ.com (October 10, 2014): http://www.tmz.com/2014/10/10/dj-quik-ghosts-tupac-karen-carpenter-studio-tmz-tv/ (last accessed 11/17/2017).

3. David Konjoyan, "Yesterday Once More: An Exclusive *HITS* Interview with Richard Carpenter" (1994). Reprinted in *Yesterday Once More: The*

Carpenters Reader, ed. Randy L. Schmidt (Chicago: Chicago Review Press, 2012), 294.

4. Ibid.

5. Ray Coleman, "Carpenters—Good, Clean, All-American Aggro!," in *Melody Maker*, 1975. Reprinted in *Yesterday Once More: The Carpenters Reader*, 166.

6. Elizabeth Freeman, *Time Binds: Queer Temporalities, Queer Histories* (Durham, NC: Duke University Press, 2010).

7. Eric Lott, "Perfect Is Dead: Karen Carpenter, Theodor Adorno, and the Radio, or If Hooks Could Kill," in *Pop When the World Falls Apart: Music in the Shadow of Doubt*, ed. Eric Weisbard (Durham, NC: Duke University Press, 2012), 62–81. Mitchell Morris, *The Persistence of Sentiment: Display and Feeling in the Popular Music of the 1970s* (Berkeley and Los Angeles: University of California Press, 2013), 118–142.

8. As Berlant explains in an interview about her book *Cruel Optimism*: "In all of these scenes of 'the good life,' the object that you thought would bring happiness becomes an object that deteriorates the conditions for happiness. But its presence represents *the possibility of happiness as such*. And so losing the bad object might be deemed worse than being destroyed by it. That's a relation of cruel optimism." "Lauren Berlant on Her Book *Cruel Optimism*," *Rorotoko*, June 5, 2013, http://rorotoko.com/interview/20120605_berlant_lauren_on_cruel_optimism.